Lind,

I hope that you enjoy this story about your Great, great, great, great Grandmother, Sarah Eliza Agassiz.

Love from,
Aunt Joan
Christmas, 2014

MUTE SWAN

The Life of
Sarah Eliza Agassiz
1806 – 1884

Patricia M. Holliss

Copyright © Patricia M. Holliss, 2014
All Rights Reserved.
No part of this publication may be reproduced except by permission of the copyright holder.
The right of Patricia M. Holliss to be identified as the Author of this Work has been asserted by her in accordance with the Copyright, Designs and Patents Act 1988.

First published in 2014 by Patricia M. Holliss
Cover Design by Samuel J. Holliss

Printed by CreateSpace, an Amazon.com Company
Available on Kindle and other devices

For my Mother, Grandmothers and Great Grandmothers:

You shaped my world and made it a better place.

1 Sarah Eliza Agassiz

CONTENTS

Introduction 9

1 The Timber Merchant 13

2 The Brewer 25

3 The Brewer's Children 35

4 The Gentlemen Farmers 43

5 The Londoners 48

6 The Village Gossip 55

7 The Lovers 65

8 The Bride 77

9 The Newly Weds 85

10 The Travellers 91

11 The Travellers Return 103

12 Ach Tannenbaum 118

13 The Matron 133

14 The Mourners 145

15 The Widow 151

16 The Grandmother 157

17 Old Age 168

18 The Memory 181

Illustrations 183

Bibliography 184

Notes 185

Introduction

As the train neared the station it slowed down to a crawling pace. Carriages shuddered and jerked along the last few yards of rail, signaling the scramble for coats and scarves to begin. The final jolt bumped me out of my seat. Flinging a backpack over my shoulder, I joined the purposeful throng that spilled forth into the colossal, echoing cavity of Waterloo Station. Once outside, the wave of pedestrian traffic was abandoned by turning east towards Upper Ground, a street that edges the bank of the Thames River. That day, a line of delivery vans snaked along the wide, well-serviced road, past the National Theatre. The traffic sidled slowly around orange cones, cranes and construction-site barriers.

Brothels, bear-baiting dens, taverns and gaming parlours once clamoured for business along Upper Ground. It is one of the oldest streets in the district. When Blackfriars Bridge was constructed to connect the swampy margins of the south bank to London City in 1769, it became a place where fortunes were to be made by those willing to venture risk. Industry soon took the place of the less-salubrious ventures. A profusion of foundries, timber yards, windmills and wharves rose along the riverside. Upper Ground, historically known for its lack of amenities, was the muddy, rutted track that linked those various dealings.[1]

Taking a turning from Upper Ground towards the Embankment, the City's landmarks came into view. On that miserably dreary day, they were not my object. What I was seeking were the ancient watermen's steps that mark the position of the Tudor's royal barge-house. Looking down to the river's edge, the slimy green cobbles were just visible in the low-tide mud, tumbling untidily down into the water.

Those familiar with London might wonder at the significance of a few stones on the edge of the Thames. The 'barge-house steps', with the OXO tower that rises next to them, mark this story's beginning. Between these two points once stood the timber yard that belonged to Robert Nicholson, the grandfather of Sarah Eliza Agassiz, and my fifth Great Grandfather.[2]

Born in 1806, Sarah Eliza Nunn's life began towards the end of the Georgian period. Her childhood spanned the Regency and she lived through a significant portion of Queen Victoria's reign – a time that marked momentous social, industrial and economic changes in England.

Sarah Eliza became the wife of Lewis Agassiz, Esquire, of Stour Lodge.[3] While researching the life of this gentleman, it became apparent that the dusty documents of Britain's archives reveal the details of men's lives rather than those of women. There is little evidence to be found pertaining to Sarah Eliza, mother to thirteen of Lewis's children. Her history, as with that of other women of the past, is elusive.

> *What shares have women in the history of men? We hear of empresses and queens, of heroines and geniuses, and even of those women who won a perilous fame through the power of loveliness or surpassing grace; but woman in the peace and quiet beauty of her domestic life, in the gentleness of her love ... we must not hope to find.*[4]

The dearth of information about Sarah Eliza's life suggests insignificance, a Victorian attitude towards women generally, rather than one of today. Sarah Eliza Agassiz was a woman whose existence remains unmentioned in history books, but her life was far from insignificant.

Some of her experiences may be encountered in her husband's travel journal.[5] That is a tale describing long distances travelled in a barely comfortable carriage. Sarah Eliza accompanied Lewis on the journey but how she managed the daily demands of tiny children and dirty nappies can only be imagined.

What was her life really like? What were the practicalities of her world? How did she respond to the trials and hardships of everyday challenges? Though she never captured headlines, she must have been a formidable lady. The practicalities of Sarah Eliza's world were both similar and dissimilar to those of women today. They are interesting and worthy of recording. Sarah Eliza's story reveals the impact women can make on the world in which they live. Her influence will continue as it already has, for generations to come.

Various feminine accounts of the long nineteenth century remain. Well-to-do women of the time recorded the events of their lives in letters, journals and scrapbooks. Sarah Eliza would have done so herself, however, it seems these traces of her life have been lost. One day such accounts may be uncovered to reveal the real-life woman. Until they do, the details of her story must largely be left to the imagination.

This sketch of an ordinary middle class woman's journey through life is rich in factual material. It is based on archival information, which has been intertwined with the journals and historical descriptions of others. Though the story's characters were all real people with a place and purpose in history, their personalities and responses are fiction, based where possible, on snippets gleaned from written evidence.

Readers, please forgive the assumptions made. It is supposition that Sarah Eliza's feminine responsibilities and cares were similar to those of other women of her times. There is no doubt that she was a real person, with her own quirks and peculiarities. Describing a personality is essentially a subjective process and consequently readers will reach their own conclusions about Sarah Eliza's character. I hope any questions and doubts that are raised by this account will challenge others to further investigation.

My grateful thanks must be offered to my friends and family – all those who have read this work for errors and provided suggestions

Introduction

to improve it. I appreciated the recollections of Granny Barnes shared by my mother and aunts. Particular recognition must be made of the contributions of my cousin, John Barker, for his thoughts and influence. John's publication of the life of Lewis Agassiz supplied many of the details used as background for this story. Thank you to the helpful, friendly services provided at the archive centres around England. Without their assistance very little of our family history would ever be known.

1 The Timber Merchant

In 1798, Nicholson's Yard was a mucky, chaotic shambles perched on the mudflats of a tidal river. Hoists and cranes crowded along the water's edge amongst the cluttered moorings of skiffs and unwieldy barges. Above the high water mark, logs were heaped in precariously balanced stacks. Further back in the yard stood a warehouse. The large open-sided shelter had a lean-to workshop attached to it. There were several deep-dug sawpits located outside. Though lined and posted with rough-hewn planks, the bases of those ditches squelched with mud. There was a stable further beyond, with huge carts leaning together on the roadside, ready to transport the timber onwards.

Robert Nicholson managed his various business ventures from an office above the warehouse. This day, as every other, the entrepreneur had been at his work since dawn. Distracted from his ledgers by a loud noise outside, Robert paused and blotted his page. He laid aside his spectacles and rubbed his eyes. The figures on the page were growing blurry in the low light of early evening. Robert took out his handkerchief and wiped his forehead, noticing too late an ugly black ink spot smeared across the white cloth.

"It's time to give up for the day," Robert muttered to himself. "I mustn't forget my meeting."

It had been a hot sultry day but it would cool now that the sun was going down. Small wherries and sailboats bobbed past along the river, the lowering sun highlighting their sails. As usual, there was plenty of traffic on the water and it would continue until well after darkness engulfed the city.

1 The Timber Merchant

Southwark's proximity to the naval re-victualing yards at Deptford and various shipbuilding enterprises greatly benefited local entrepreneurs during the French wars. Consequently, with his wood trade situated so ideally, on the banks of the Thames, Robert Nicholson became a wealthy man within a few years – a very rich man. Self-made men like Robert were gradually making their own place in society. The class orders of the Georgian Era were being challenged by the prosperity of such gentlemen.

Familiar workday sounds penetrated the thin walls, calling Robert's attention to the flurry of activity beneath his window. Looking down Robert could see that his men below were labouring hard, steadfastly off-loading timber at the water's edge. This was the busiest time of year. Ships arrived every week from the north over the long days of summer. There was plenty to keep the men busy. Winches and pulleys strained and creaked under awkward loads as the logs swung from the clumsy barge via cranes to the riverbank.

The largest and best quality trunks, which arrived from the Baltic's vast forests, would be shifted to the shipbuilder's yard next door almost as soon as they were landed. Any timber suitable for masts was highly prized.

The smaller logs would be consigned to the sawpits for trimming, before being purchased by the local building trade. The staves, off cuts and short ends, were destined for the cooper's yard to be shaped into casks and barrels.

"Steady as she goes. Not too fast now!"

There were shouts as a log swung wide and men grappled in the knee-deep mire to balance it.

"Watch out Jack, keep your head low! Hey, you there, keep your eyes on the job!"

Down in the warehouse, he could see sweat glistening on the backs of the hewers as they strove to finish their day's work too, racing against the encroaching darkness that would soon impede their sawpit exertions. Working the yard was a dangerous occupation, requiring close attention, as well as substantial strength.

1 The Timber Merchant

Robert was familiar with the physical demands of such labour from his youth but he was too old for such effort now. Reluctantly he dragged his eyes away. Overseeing the men was the foreman's job not his own and Robert had to be content with that.

Time was short and there were more pressing matters to be considered that evening. A glance at his pocket watch reminded Robert that it was time to depart the security of his office. Town coat donned and buttoned, he took the narrow staircase down into the sawdust-filled gloom of the workshop. Nodding at his men, he was relieved to emerge into the relatively fresher air outside. Robert had an arrangement to meet his friends at a Cornhill coffee house.

He considered for a moment whether to hail a chair but decided against it. It was faster to travel London by foot.

2 London seen from Blackfriars Bridge, 1814

Robert turned to the east, to pass the iron foundry next door to the yard. When he mounted the steps to Blackfriars Bridge, two small, grubby lads approached carrying lanterns, hands outstretched to receive the penny required for lighting his way. Recalling what it

1 The Timber Merchant

was to feel hungry, Robert paid them both for the task, though there was sufficient light for walking. There was a toll, another penny to pay to cross the bridge with the wagons and horses that shared the same busy thoroughfare.

His cane tapped out a steady rhythm on the pavement as Robert strode on, barely aware of his surroundings. He ignored the familiar sight of St Paul's dome that rose majestically into the backlit sky. The blurred masts in the distance went unnoticed that evening too. Those masts belonged to the merchant ships moored across the river at Wapping. They transported spices, sugar and tobacco from distant countries, as well as his timber. Trading hoys, which brought hops, wheat and coal from rural England to the metropolis, jostled for position amongst the tall ships.

The pedestrian easily kept pace with laden carts, their wooden wheels clanking noisily along the cobbles beside him. There were ladders and precarious structures of wooden scaffolding to dodge along his route as Robert trudged uphill past the columns of Mansion House.

Soft whinnies penetrated the gloom. Horses sought to find sure footing through the mud and muck that never seemed to vanish from the streets, even in summer. Attached to assorted drays, the horses snorted impatiently as they waited for their drivers to lead them home for their evening repose.

Robert hunched over, making his way onwards. He was deep in thought, his mind completely occupied that twilight. Unusually for him, it was neither his ledgers, nor his commercial holdings that concerned him.

He was considering his wife and children, and their futures. Robert's family was special to him and their security important.' If anything untoward happened to him, he wanted to ensure that his loved ones were well provided for.

Since he could not determine fate, finalising his will was the concern of the evening. A man such as Robert, who had reached the age of fifty, was fortunate but his death would be the gravest thing

1 The Timber Merchant

that could happen to his daughters. There was reason to be worried. At the end of the eighteenth century, London was an unhealthy place to live. For the city's million inhabitants, whether beggar, merchant or baronet, life expectancy was short.

Overcrowding, the lack of a clean water supply, as well as an inadequate drainage system, all combined to make infectious disease an unavoidable fact of life. Though smallpox was on the decrease, epidemics of typhoid and typhus waxed and waned, along with annual outbreaks of measles, influenza and scarlet fever. Consumption accounted for a third of deaths in London at this time. No one was immune. It was wise to be prepared.

The lawyer had drafted the document under Robert's instructions. He had chosen the executors carefully. George Wolff was an upright, religious man, trustworthy in all things.[2] His friendship was crucial to Robert's dealings in Baltic timber. Norwegian by birth, Wolff was the consul of Denmark and Norway. Robert held him in great esteem. George, he knew would continue to advise his family on business matters.

The other executor, Richard Pape, was Robert's favoured broker. Robert's solicitor from Borough High Street, on the south side of the river, was to convene with them at the Bank Coffeehouse, their usual place for doing business. Being a man of figures, Robert planned to ensure his instructions were clearly understood.

Robert had discussed his plans with his wife. After twenty-four years of marriage, he expected her companionship and inquisition at the end of each day. Though it was usually late when his carriage rolled up the gravel driveway, Sarah was always waiting to greet him.

"I want to be fair to them all Sarah," he had told her the night before. "There will be no difference in their shares, sons or daughters," he knew that he had her approval, in the equal treatment of their children.

"If you want Young Robert and Frederick to take on the yard, they'll require a sound financial backing to get started. You'll need to leave substantial capital tied into the business for them." Despite the social disadvantages of her gender, Sarah had always tried to understand the complexities of Robert's occupation. Trusting her judgements, he never discouraged her from voicing her opinions and often sought her advice.

"They know the business affairs well enough. They are both quite ready to step into my shoes. I don't think they'll need propping up." That his two eldest sons, Robert and Frederick, were content to take on his timber yard gave him great satisfaction. Young Robert was already learning the trade and Frederick was soon to be apprenticed to a builder, an educational experience that would be of great advantage to the family establishment.[3]

"I'm pleased that you've settled James Henry in a position," Sarah continued. "That was money well-spent." The young man had just been apprenticed to a surgeon on St Margaret's Hill in Southwark.[4] After serving the seven year term as apothecary apprentice, James hoped to take a position at the adjacent St Thomas's Hospital.

"Yes, it is fortunate that he has such a passion for healing, since two is enough to manage the timber business. I'm glad he has ambition and purpose."

"I wonder where Edward's choices will lie." Edward was their youngest, a tiny child. It was too soon to see what direction Edward would choose.

Then there was their home to settle. He assured Sarah that their house would be hers for life, as long as she required it.

"I will need a good income to maintain myself and the younger children here, Robert. You will make sure we are provided for, in case anything happens, won't you?"

"I've taken advice on that. £600 a year, raised from the estate, should be enough for you to keep several maids, two manservants, a good cook, and a carriage and team. You'll still live in style, my dear."

"How will you provide for our five daughters? They will need a worthwhile settlement if they are to find suitable husbands."

1 The Timber Merchant

"There will be £2000 for each of them on my demise with a further £3000 to be their marriage portion. Louise is still a child, but yes I suppose the older ones will soon be looking for husbands." He paused to consider the prospect.

"Nevertheless, I am reluctant they should marry too young."

"Better they wait," Sarah nodded. "Twenty-six seems a good age to me. That was the age I was when I married you. Let them enjoy the comforts and security of home before they plunge into the cares of matrimony and motherhood."

"They'll be quite sensible and able to make sound decisions by then."

"Today, with the heat, I was reminded of my youth, spent sweating in the ship-building yards over at Wapping. I'm pleased the life my children lead is so different. Thinking of childhood reminded me to include something for my sister Dinah and also my uncle who still lives up in York."

"All your hard work has paid off Robert. I'm proud of what you've achieved. Father would never have allowed me to marry a penniless boy with a northern accent."

"Hard work, and a great deal of providence too, Sarah. You know, I can barely remember York. Life has changed so much for me Sarah."

Robert established his first yard in Southwark, just opposite the Marshalsea Prison. That was before he married Miss Sarah Hawes in 1774.[5] By the age of twenty-seven, he had the means to support a wife in comfort. Sarah's father, Thomas Hawes, was a well-respected gentleman, who expected his daughter to be amply provided for.[6]

"We've been blessed to raise such a large family too. I know it hasn't been easy Sarah, we've had our losses, like everyone else, but we've still reason to be thankful."

Sarah and Robert had nine living children, including their youngest, Edward. Three sons died as infants. Three sons survived childhood. Young Robert, Frederick, and James Henry were living

1 The Timber Merchant

in the family home as well as their five daughters, Sarah Hawes, Ann, Harriot, Amelia and Louisa.[7]

Robert and Sarah's firstborn son died shortly after his birth. Their second child was baptised in 1776, at the family church of St George the Martyr, Southwark. The births of more daughters followed. By the time their sons, Robert and Frederick, were born, Robert's business was situated at Falcon Yard near to their family home in Adam's Place, off Borough High Street. He purchased the Upper Ground Yard around 1790 at the onset of the French troubles.

Then in April 1796, Robert acquired a prime piece of real estate five miles south of Southwark, on Loam Pit Hill, the road leading from Deptford towards Lewisham.[8] Sarah may not have known precisely how wealthy her husband was but she was well aware that the purchase of a country house was an outward sign of her husband's status. Robert Nicholson, Esquire, had justifiably earned his title.

When Robert, keen to show his purchase to his wife, took her to Lewisham in his barouche within a few days of his purchase, Sarah was reserved in her response. She suspected that Robert might have exaggerated the virtues of their new abode in his excitement.

"I am certain you will appreciate this place Sarah."

"I hope it's not too large, Robert, you know how draughty those big stone houses can be. They are well known for being impossible to heat properly."

"There will be plenty of servants to keep the home warm and clean. And there's a well-appointed coach house too, enough room for two fine carriages and their teams." Robert had kept his own stables at his premises in Southwark for decades.

"It will no longer be acceptable for you and the girls to drive yourselves. You'll have a liveried groom. That will be in keeping with living in such a fine place."

His suggestion impressed Sarah – keeping a liveried groom was a socially significant step to take.

1 The Timber Merchant

"Of course I'll keep my own man to drive me to my business appointments so yours is always free to transport you to your engagements across the river."

Their new home, Stone House, was a mansion designed and built as an architect's own private residence twenty years prior to Nicholson taking possession of it.[9] Gibson was a gentleman architect. It could be said that he enjoyed the finer things of life – his claret, art and music – rather than rummaging around building sites. Consequently this, Gibson's finest and most expensive work to date was luxurious, if not a little eccentric. For a time the house was called the 'Comical House' due to its oddly unbalanced appearance.

3 Stone House. Used with the kind permission of Deptford Local History and Archives Centre

A square villa, it had three bay windows, one on each of three sides, with a large columned portico on the remaining flank. The entrance opened into a central, stone-floored, octagonal hall.

21

1 The Timber Merchant

A grand staircase dominated the hall, which was top-lit from a lantern gallery high above. In addition to the interior view down into the lobby from the lantern, there was a sweeping panorama to be admired across Greenwich: the view stretched beyond the Thames towards the City and the dome of St Paul's Cathedral. The gardens of the Stone House were extensive and ornate.[10]

"Our children will be introduced to society from here." Robert told his wife as he gazed over his newly acquired property. "Our genteel daughters will enjoy their daily fresh air exercise along these ambling paths with their equally refined friends."

"It's beautiful – a home for entertaining, for wooing and for weddings, for balls, baptisms and banquets. Quite a dream come true Robert." Sarah loved her new home.

Suitors began to call on the family the summer they moved to the countryside. The daughters of Robert Nicholson were clearly heiresses which made them worthy of seeking acquaintance. One successful caller was Thomas Dowley, the son of a wealthy corn and coal merchant of Bankside. When Thomas married Sarah, Robert's eldest daughter in 1799, she was twenty-three, a little younger than the age her parents had agreed upon. Her sister, Ann, and Thomas's brother, James, witnessed the marriage at the Church of St Paul's in Deptford, as did their respective fathers. James Dowley was later to marry Harriot.

With the move to Lewisham, Robert became one of London's early commuters – he lived in the countryside and travelled the five miles to Southwark to work each day.

Later that same year, Sarah warned her husband, as he set off for the city one morning.

"Do be careful where you go. I have heard that the typhus and scarlet fever have reached epidemic proportions across the water."

"I'll stay in the office Sarah, I promise. I don't want to bring disease home. No coffeehouse meetings for the time being."

"And remember not to eat out, even on the south bank. I'll make sure you have provisions from the kitchen."

1 The Timber Merchant

Despite their precautions, Robert's precious youngest son died in November. Edward's burial took place just days before his fifth birthday.

The epidemic continued to rage through winter. Robert, the eldest son, had just attained his majority when he died a month later in December. Sarah and Robert Nicholson's first grandchild was born that Christmas of 1799. The birth of such a sickly child was small joy to a family in deep mourning.

Heartbroken, Robert lost interest in his business activities. His health suffered. The medical profession subjected the ailing gentleman to a variety of treatments which included cupping as well as bleeding him. All that they could offer for his pain were opiates. Robert's anxiety to finalise his will proved well founded. He died at the end of May 1800.[11]

Robert's executors and solicitors faced the arduous task of ordering his business affairs and executing the meticulous details of his will. The London newspapers were soon advertising Robert's holdings for sale as the family's inheritance was consolidated.

His properties in Cross Street and Finsbury Place were advertised: six houses near Finsbury Square, four in Castle Street and twelve in York Court. There were assets in Webber Street, Charles Street and St Georges Row as well as two parcels of freehold land at Battersea. The sale of the Adam's Place houses followed, along with two dwellings, one in Brompton and one in Knightsbridge.[12]

Robert had long since moved on from being a timber merchant. He was a property developer with a knack for recognising an investment opportunity.

The Gentleman's Magazine honoured him with an obituary:

Mr Nicholson of Loam Pit Hill, Deptford and of Christchurch Surrey was a timber merchant. He had by business of near 40 years standing, accumulated a very large fortune and had lately lost two of his sons, one 21 years old, the other an infant.[13]

23

2 The Brewer

Born the son of a gentleman farmer, Thomas Nunn was seventeen when he decided he preferred a city life. His parents had anticipated that, as their eldest, he would help to manage the family land.[1] Instead, his father reluctantly accepted Thomas's lack of interest in the farming enterprises of his forebears and established his son in London.

"It's the way of young people today," the elder Thomas Nunn looked sagely at his be-wigged friend. Golding Constable, who lived in a village close to the Nunn's farm, nodded.[2]

"I've much the same problem with my eldest son too. John has his heart set on becoming an artist of all things. He wants to go to London to study. Really, I do think painting an unsuitable occupation for a gentleman. I've insisted he stay here to manage the coal dealership."

"I believe there's money to be made in brewing. Yes, that will be a fitting alternative for my son and heir. One of the fellows I hunt with suggested it. Osgood Hanbury set his son Samson up in the brewing industry a decade ago. It's been a successful enterprise for his family." Indeed, brewing was a highly prosperous and secure occupation for a young man with the capital to invest.[3]

Thomas was duly established as a partner in a London porter and ale business in 1796.[4] Within six years, the young man was able to expand his concerns to invest in a partnership with the highly successful brewing company owned by the Calvert family.[5]

He threw himself wholeheartedly into learning all he could about brewing by joining the Brewers' Guild. Instead of serving the required seven-year apprenticeship, 'Thomas Nunn (jun.), son of Thomas Nunn of Lawford House, Essex, was admitted as a Freeman of the City in the Company of Brewers, by redemption'. 'Cloathed' on the same day, he became a full voting member of the London Livery.[6] Before long, Thomas Nunn (jun.) was elected to the Court of Assistants to serve on the governing body of the Company of Brewers.[7] Thomas's business partners were also prominent members of the Court of Assistants.

Once established in a respectable livery company, Thomas enjoyed the prospect of financial security. In addition to his own business, he stood to inherit a share of his father's various farming and financial enterprises. Thomas was free to contemplate marriage.

Being an eligible bachelor, there were plenty of invitations for Thomas to attend social engagements. The dance floor remained one of the few places a young man could make the acquaintance of respectable young ladies. Dancing was a pleasant social activity, enjoyed by many, both at private parties and at public venues.[8] Country dances, Scottish flings, quadrilles and cotillions – these frolics constituted a popular evening's entertainment.

Many promising young women were introduced to Thomas that year. From amongst them the twenty-three year old heir was free to make his choice of a wife. However, it was not a decision to be ruled solely by his heart. Thomas had family obligations to consider – his marriage needed to contribute to their wealth and prestige. Thomas was expected to engage in a 'prudent romance'.[9] With this in mind, his father arranged that his son made the acquaintance of George Wolff, a business associate of one of Thomas Nunn's Lawford neighbours.[10]

Amongst the multitude of diaphanous muslins that Thomas Nunn partnered around the ballrooms of London during the season of 1802, Ann Nicholson became the lady who caught his particular attention. She was beautiful, accomplished, and rich. Yet she also carried herself with an appealing grace and unaffected modesty. The pair met at George Wolffe's home in Streatham.

2 The Brewer

The first two dances that evening were energetic and fast-paced *contredans anglaises*. Those capers soon rendered the enthusiastic company eager to partake of the iced refreshments that graced the trays of Wolff's footmen.

George Wolff took it upon himself as host, to introduce Thomas to the daughter of his deceased friend during the interlude.

"Come now Thomas, we can't have you buried in the card room. I've a better plan for your evening. You're expected to fulfil your obligations as a dancing partner and the matrons will be wishing to make your acquaintance, besides." George continued talking as they wended their way past fluttering fans and across the overly warm room.

"I have heard it said that 'a single man in possession of a good fortune must be in want of a wife'. Now that's a reference particularly apt for a young gentleman such as you."[11] Thomas inadvertently slipped his finger inside his neck cloth, suddenly feeling the oppressive temperature of the room.

Ann was seated on a plush chaise next to her mother and sisters. She wore a Grecian style robe trimmed with velvet and gossamer net, dainty slippers to match. Upon introduction, Thomas took her gloved hand as expected and bowed low, ankles together, legs straight.

"May I request the pleasure of your company for the cotillion Miss Nicholson? Perhaps you would permit me to write my name on your dance card?" She shyly flicked her fan and nodded in response. With the evident endorsement of her father's trusted friend, the young woman could not refuse. Her mother beamed her encouragement.

"Pray take a seat with us and tell us something of the countryside Mr Nunn." Sarah had already determined that Thomas was not a Londoner. That was no impediment. George had given good account of the young man's prospects and upon hearing the trustworthy gentleman's approbation of Mr Nunn's character she was pleased to nurture Thomas's attentions to her daughter.

4 A Regency Ball Dress, Ackermann's Repository

    Ann's hand rested lightly in Thomas's as they took their place in the set. He had rehearsed a few phrases that might begin a polite conversation suitable for the occasion.

    "Private balls are so much more pleasant than public ones."[12]

"And Balham is a lovely situation for a ball, don't you agree sir?"

"Mr Wolff is always an excellent host, I think."

"We enjoy the most entertaining parties here."

Thomas tried to avoid contemplating the modest lace *fichu* that covered her décolletage as they performed the figures of the cotillion together. He wondered if his unrefined country ways would offend the delicate sensitivities of this elegant, London bred girl. Ann responded to his attention with a demure smile.

The delicate curve of her lips was enough to encourage his pursuit, but did not reveal her teeth – or a fluttering heart. Ann knew her romantic dreams and feelings were of little importance. Her mother had made it clear where her duty lay.

Introduction to a gentleman at a ball did not mean that a young lady could assume an acquaintance with him. Therefore, before the evening ended, Ann's mother invited Thomas to call at their home later in the week, thus ensuring an ongoing contact.

In addition to filial obedience, protocol, dress and etiquette were important in all social undertakings in that era. There was a strict unwritten code of conduct that was unwise, if not impossible, to flout. Class was well-defined, the levels of society divided into a distinct hierarchy.

Ann and Thomas did not pretend to be members of the Quality. They lacked the connections for that. Ann came from a merchant background, and while Thomas's family were ranked as provincial gentility, he was not upper class. He earned his living as a brewer. The couple's social standing was termed polite. It did not admit them to royalty and limited their access to London's more exclusive functions such as those held at Almack's Reception Rooms.

Still, London held many forms of entertainment acceptable to the respectable classes. There were plenty of social engagements where young people could meet. Ann and Thomas's friendship developed and became more intimate.

On a damp dark day, the deepest of winter, two young men stood waiting at the altar rail. They were smartly turned out in elegant beaver hats, neck cloths, well-cut tailcoats and top-boots. Inside, the church was not much warmer than outside, and it was definitely dimmer. The shadows were barely relieved by candle flame – the Rector was sparing in the number he lit for such a small family affair.

Accompanying Thomas was his friend, a young Oxford scholar by the name of George Way. He was standing witness in place of a member of Thomas's family.[13] Ann, as for other such young women of her times, had accepted the direction of her mother in making her choices and accepted Thomas's marriage proposal.

Frederick offered his arm to his bonneted sister as he handed her down from the carriage. Ann shivered. Frederick smiled down at her encouragingly, wondering if it was trepidation, or cold, that affected her. He pragmatically decided the trembling was unremarkable considering the fashionably flimsy frock that she wore underneath her pelisse.

Though her long woollen coat covered her from neck to toe, her tremors continued. At least her gloved hands were warm. Ann handed her muff to her sister and took his arm. She was glad of her family's support as she walked down the aisle of St Paul's Church, in Deptford, to say her wedding vows.[14]

The newly married couple settled into a large mansion in Cripplegate.[15] Their home was situated near the top end of Red Cross Street where it connected with Fore Street. It was close to the ancient pile of St Giles's Church. From the church's picturesque tower, melodic chimes rang out the hour and heralded the commencement of weddings, funerals and Sunday services.

The hubbub of Red Cross Street was typical of London streets. For Ann, it seemed a noisy place to live compared to the seclusion of Loam Pit Hill. Hawkers called their wares and the ragman clunked back and forth with his handcart. A milkmaid stopped at the end of the street with her cow and stool every few days. Flocks of sheep, on their way to slaughter, added to the unsavoury atmosphere of Cripplegate's streets.

This was not a quiet neighbourhood.[16]

The oyster girl visited regularly too. Thomas was fond of the native Colchester oysters that arrived every week from Essex. Ann considered them a little common for her dainty tastes.

What was even worse for Ann, than the noise of church bells and street vendors, was that their dwelling backed onto the Peacock Brewery yard.[17] The small outdoor space behind the house was not a pleasant place to spend any time. All manner of noises, including bad language and constant banging, emanated from the brewery: not to mention the pungent odours. The cloying smell of malt and boiling hops were ghastly in summer. It was all immeasurably different to the pleasantly manicured garden in which Ann was used to taking her daily exercise.

Mary Ann Nunn, named for Thomas's mother, was baptised in December 1803. Thomas and Ann celebrated the birth of a son just fourteen months later. Then, towards the end of 1805, when baby Tom was only a few months old, Ann realised that she was expecting again.

Feeling tired and fragile, she penned a fraught letter to her mother. Ann was terrified at the prospect of another confinement so soon after the last. Her mother understood her fears and agreed with her daughter about the dangers Ann's family was exposed to, living in such a dubious area. Sarah Nicholson replied by the return post.

> *Please consider removing yourself from the disease-ridden miasma's of Cripplegate and come out to Loam Pit Hill for your lying-in. I am sure that Mr Nunn will agree with the sense of this. It would be much better for your health and your children's. I would so enjoy seeing the little ones for Christmas. It is time they met their cousins. You will be very comfortable here. We will have such a merry time.*

Ann was not sure how she was going to convince her husband but she desperately wanted to accept her mother's invitation to spend winter amongst the comforts and space of Stone House.

"It's not that our home is uncomfortable, Thomas." She was on the defensive as she tried to explain her decision to her husband.

"I'm just so tired of the city. I miss Loam Pit Hill, the open air, the views, the walks. Here, it's cramped and confined and there's nowhere to take exercise."

She threw herself down on the chaise with a loud sigh, trying not to whine.

"For I can hardly loiter in the street, not unless you are free to escort me," she continued. "So to be honest I feel a little trapped. And I really would appreciate being with Mother for a while."

Ann wanted Thomas to understand how much her life had altered since her marriage. She missed the companionship of her sisters and her social life had diminished drastically. There were still card evenings and afternoon visits from a few friends but her seemingly perpetual state of pregnancy excluded any dancing.

"Sarah is too busy with her own family to visit me here. Louise and Harriot are distracted by ribbons and bonnets, not to mention their endless rounds of tea parties, soirees and balls."

"I do understand my dear, but I would rather we were together. You know I can't accompany you; I have obligations at the brewery and of course my guild meetings to attend."

"You will be free for the season's hunts down in Essex, if I am with Mother." Ann knew that was one temptation Thomas could not resist.

So it was agreed that, before the Christmas season began, Ann would take her children across the river. On a chilly autumn day, she climbed carefully aboard the coach, wearing 'a little muslin poke, a sweet smile and an immense protuberance,' trying her best to be graceful.[18] Her nursemaid accompanied her with the wriggling Tom in her arms and little Mary.

The carriage jogged past St Giles, across London Bridge and within the hour, they were slowing down for the steep ascent towards Stone House. The barouche swung around the semi-circular drive and pulled up outside the familiar, out-sized portico.

2 The Brewer

The pleasant hush of the countryside permeated her mood. Ann felt quite at peace.

"It's so good to be Home." She breathed deeply and smiled. "No menus to plan, no housemaids to oversee, no tradesmen's bills to pay," were the thoughts that lit up her face. In this luxurious place there were fires in all the bedrooms, a multitude of servants, and a good cook. There was no noise from the street and no bad smells either. Ann could relax and let nurse take charge of the children.

The cares and responsibilities of motherhood had lifted for a time. Ann hummed as she stroked her beloved pianoforte, looking forward to spending time indulging in her music, with the hope that Mother would finish the layette for the new baby.

Nelson's state funeral and the grand procession down the Thames went unnoticed by Ann in her blissful bloated state that January. Ann's child was born on 17 February 1806, a month after that big national event.[19] Her eldest daughter, Mary, was 26 months old and Thomas a year.

The birth was not easy. It quite exhausted Ann, leaving her poorly and frail. The doctor who attended her spoke quietly to her mother and husband.

"Mrs Nunn should make every effort to avoid having more children. I fear this birth has caused irreparable damage and a further pregnancy could well be fatal."

A month later, she was barely well enough to present Sarah Eliza Nunn for baptism at St Giles Church. Ann's health deteriorated steadily through May and the decline continued into June. Thomas failed to attend the meetings of the Court of Assistants for those two months. He was at the bedside of his young wife. By then it was clear that she was not going to survive. Ann died four months after Eliza's birth. The family had her interred alongside her father and brothers in the family vault at St Paul's, Deptford.[20]

Thomas continued to live at Red Cross Street after his wife's death. A nurse, carefully overseen by his mother-in-law, cared for

2 The Brewer

the three infants. They did not lack for adult attention, and they had each other for company. Games were played, laughter was heard, and their father was always there to say goodnight.

When the Peacock Brewery closed its doors and advertised the sale of its team of dray horses in 1810, Thomas Nunn (jun.) decided it was time he moved his family back to Essex. He was a familiar face around the Stour Valley, for Thomas had invested in several properties adjacent to his father's land in Lawford, shortly after Ann's death. Thomas Nunn (sen.) managed the properties for his son until such time as he was able to do so himself.[21]

The older gentleman had continued to add to his own estate during Thomas's years in London and made improvements to Lawford House. By the time his son contemplated moving, Thomas Nunn (sen.) had ventured into the banking world.

3 The Brewer's Children

Eliza was still a young child when the family moved from the house in Red Cross Street. The children were woken early one fresh autumn morning. Dressed in warm layers, despite the promise of a balmy day, they were bundled into the carriage with their nurse. The stage-coach bound for Harwich departed London at 6.45am.

Being harvest time, the sweet scent of freshly mown hay began to penetrate the interior of the coach within a few miles of setting out. The girls were wide-eyed and very excited. These were their first views of the gently undulating farmlands of Essex. Teams of smocked workers in battered hats swarmed across the fields, wielding sickles and forks, tossing straw high up onto hayricks. Compared to their confined London world, what lay before the children was a magical green and gold vista of rolling meadowlands and broad open spaces.

By the time they reached their destination, the family had endured a long day's drive. Lawford was fifty-seven miles from London. They had to stop periodically, every ten to fifteen miles, for the necessary change of horses in the small market towns that dotted their route; Romford, Brentwood and Chelmsford, then Witham. Colchester had been the last change, just seven miles past.

Twilight was approaching when Grandfather Nunn set out with his groom to meet the London coach on the Colchester Road. It would pass on the outskirts of Lawford. The elderly gentleman eased himself out of his carriage and peered down the lane, squinting into the sunset. He leaned on his cane and hoped they would arrive before dark.

3 The Brewer's Children

Thomas Nunn (sen.) had not met his London granddaughters. His wife reminded him that Mary would be six now, and Eliza four. By his son's proud reports, they were vivacious and pretty, well on their way to becoming accomplished young women.

"Though I do hope that's true, they're a little too young to expect too much of just yet." Their Grandmother Nunn had read her son's intelligences with pleasure.

Grandfather Nunn was more familiar with his grandson Tom, who had previously visited Essex on a number of occasions with his father. Tom pleased his grandfather enormously by showing an interest in the family's holdings despite his youth. It wasn't long before the lad learned to ride well enough to keep up with the men on their farm rounds, even though he was still on a little pony. Thomas Nunn chuckled suddenly as he waited.

"Young Tom's a handful isn't he?" The grandfather reflected his thoughts to his groomsman, for want of any other company to talk to that evening.

"He's turning out to be a fine, strapping laddie Sir, you must be proud of him."

"Do you remember how he pleaded to learn to handle a gun? I think he tried to convince you to teach him in secret didn't he?"

Thomas Nunn (sen.) was contemplating having a family portrait done of them all. His neighbour, George Bridges, had a splendid family portrait in his dining room.[1] Thomas regularly admired the work while enjoying a glass of claret with his friend of an evening.[2] Thomas (sen.) wondered if he could arrange a sitting for his son's young brood. Something of his home in the background or perhaps the towers of Mistley Church would make a fine backdrop to a painting.[3] He was not sure that the young man, who had done the work, was still working in the area.

George Bridges, wishing to aid the career of the fledgling artist, had offered the portrait commission to John Constable, the son of their old friend, some years prior. With preliminary sketches and frequent sittings, the project took several weeks to execute.

3 The Brewer's Children

Unfortunately, the young man seemed to have become overly fond of one of George's daughters.[4]

"I could not tolerate such behaviour," George recounted the story to his neighbour over dinner one evening, "John Constable, being but a poor artist, could not be encouraged. I had no choice but to tell the man to hurry up and complete his task."[5]

Grandfather Nunn heard the oncoming coach just as it rattled around the corner and came to a stop.

"There's young Tom. He's up with the driver of course. No doubt he's tried to convince the man to let him take the reins!"

The girls were inside. There was only interior seating for six so that space was reserved for gentlewomen and their daughters. The two little round faces that he had spotted peering out of the coach disappeared from the window. Thomas could hear them chattering as they quickly gathered up their belongings. There was a wail for a beloved doll that could not be found amidst the tangle of rugs, cushions and toys. A gentle low-pitched voice soothed the situation and the two girls appeared, tumbling down the steps to join their brother.

"Grandfather, Grandfather!" One of them rushed forward and grabbed his legs, catching him by surprise. He bent forward to return the gesture with a pat and breathed in the sweet smell of the little girl's hair.

"Well Sarah Eliza Nunn," he lifted the child in his arms, "I am pleased to make your acquaintance today!" He turned and reached out to her sister.

"And Mary Ann, welcome to you too!" The delicate softness of the little hand that he clasped in his own brought tears to his eyes. He cleared his throat and put Eliza back down on the ground so that he could address his grandson with a manly handshake.

"Come along. Let's take you home. Your Grandmother is anxious to greet you too." These bright gems were just the thing to lift Mary's spirits. The old man was pleased to have his grandchildren to visit. A house such as his could easily

37

3 The Brewer's Children

accommodate a large family. To live to see it filled with the noise and laughter of his grandchildren was a gratifying thought. The family would add a sparkle to lives that had been too quiet for too long.

Shortly after arriving in Lawford, the family celebrated Tom's breeching. For the first few years of his life, the boy was dressed as his sisters were, in frocks. From about the age of six years old, he wore a skeleton suit that comprised high-waisted breeches attached to a short, stiff jacket. Progressing from petticoats was a significant milestone in the life of the son and heir.[6]

The wider family were summoned for the celebration. Aunts, uncles and grandparents visited to fill the lad's newly acquired pockets with coins. The Nunn children were to learn that there were plenty of relatives living close by in the Stour Valley.

"Where's my favourite nephew?" Uncle Carrington arrived on his horse and swung the little boy high in the air.[7]

"Uncle, be careful! All my coins will fall out of my pockets if you do that!" The lad was in a sombre mood, quite overwhelmed by the fuss.

"Here, let me see them. Why, with all those half crowns, you could buy a pony! Here you are my boy, here's something to add to your collection." There was always a special bond between young Tom and his Uncle Carrington.[8]

As was quite the usual thing to do, a governess was added to the household to assist the nursemaid who had undertaken the care of Ann's infants in London. The governess took the main responsibility for the care of Thomas Nunn's daughters.

A genteel young lady with an acceptable level of education and refined manners, the governess supervised the children at breakfast in the nursery before taking them through their morning's lessons. Reading, writing and arithmetic were the main subjects for the youngsters. French, geography and classical studies were added as they grew older. Fashion dictated their education. Afternoons were set aside for music, needlework and drawing: young ladies were

3 The Brewer's Children

expected to be accomplished in these arts. They learned to play the pianoforte under the supervision of a visiting music master.[9]

Fashion also ordained the muslin gowns of the day. Underneath the delicate dresses, flannel petticoats added extra warmth, along with cotton pantaloons that were buttoned to a bodice and open between the legs. Girls were introduced to corsets and stays at a young age to encourage a correct posture. For special occasions they could add a slip of coloured silk underneath their muslins, with a sash to match. Aprons helped keep the dresses clean for 'at home' days, of which Mary and Eliza had plenty.

The girls were encouraged to take a daily walk for exercise, in their delicate white gowns. This was a sedate walk always undertaken with the watchful presence of their governess.

"Elegance, poise and posture girls, never forget that you are refined ladies! Don't run, don't point."

"Sarah Eliza, please smile. Always a smile, it brightens you face."

They were allowed to play a few games, but only those that enhanced good deportment and taught them to move gracefully. One such game was that of Graces. For this pursuit, the two sisters each held a pair of sticks. The sticks were used to toss and catch a wooden hoop back and forth between them. Eliza and Mary decorated their hoops with coloured silks and ribbons to match their bonnets and sashes.

Dancing lessons were another means of elegant exercise for the girls. The trip out to the dance instructor in Colchester became the highlight of each week in their otherwise sheltered existence. They practised at home in between lessons, taking care to turn their feet outwards, hold their shoulders back, and keep their heads erect, as they learned to glide about the floor gracefully. Despite the discipline and strict regime, the siblings were just as tempted to childish pranks as others of their age.

"I'm gliding Mary. Look at me! I'm gliding ever so gracefully, just like Miss Smith said to," giggled Eliza slipping along the bare floor in her stocking covered feet.

3 The Brewer's Children

"Watch out! Watch where you're going," her sister warned.

Her admonition was too late to prevent the little girl tumbling head first over a small table.

There wasn't much sympathy for the child's bruises.

"Sarah Eliza, will you ever do what you are told? You must learn to behave like a lady. Off to your room now. There will be no supper for you tonight." Grandmother Nunn could be stern at times.

"But I wanted to see Father before bed. He promised to read us a story!"

"Your father will not want to see you, I'm afraid. Not until you can deport yourself properly."

The girls were expected to spend quiet afternoons at home at their samplers, practicing the skills that would later mark them out as ladies. After the light became too dim to stitch by they were allowed to play with their dolls and miniature dolls' houses.

It took time to get used to a new grandmother and time to settle into their new country life. Their first summer walks were startling experiences. Used to the noises and crowds of the metropolis, the vast open spaces and rolling fields astounded the girls.

Though they had often watched stock being herded down the street from the safety of their drawing room in London, they were intrigued by the assortment of animals to be found in the home fields. The farmyard fascinated the girls.

"Today we fed the hens and ducks in the yard." They could hardly contain their excitement as they related their outing to their father.

"And then we saw horses, dogs, cows, goats, sheep, and pigs, Father."

"Grandmamma says they all belong to Grandfather and soon there will be lots of chicks hatching so it will be even more crowded in the hen-house."

"I like the farmyard but it smells differently out there."

"Nice smells I hope Eliza." Old Thomas could not help but involve himself in the conversation.

Eliza turned as he entered the room and gave him the curtsy she was expected to greet him with.

"Yes Grandfather, not bad smells, not like the brewery."

"I'm glad you like it Eliza, it's in your blood. The Nunn's are farmers. We have always been farmers and we don't intend to change. We depend upon agriculture for our livelihoods and upon the vagaries of the weather for our survival. It's a good life, a respectable life. Your farming roots are something you can be proud of."

5 The Cornfield by John Constable, engraving by A.W. Penrose and Co Ltd, 1897

4 The Gentlemen Farmers

Essex was a largely rural county. As much as eighty per cent of the area was cultivated as arable farmland. The productive and fertile soil could be farmed intensively with rotations of wheat, barley, oats, turnips, beans and clover. Small flocks of sheep dotted the landscape, interspersed with a few dairy herds. Near the east coast, the gently rolling clay fields of the Stour Valley were known for their exceptionally superior quality. 'Some of the finest corn land in the kingdom is to be found there'.[1]

Eliza's uncle, grandfather, and great uncles farmed substantial parts of the countryside around Mistley and the Stour Estuary. The extended family, the Carrington and Risbee relatives, were also farmers.

In rural England, those who owned property dominated. Responsible for husbanding the land, they also helped to uphold the law. They intervened in disputes and took care of the poor.

On occasion, Grandfather Nunn took Eliza and Mary for rides through the little villages. There were no crowds to be seen but the people they did meet seemed very friendly. Grandfather was well known in the district. He had many business acquaintances as well as numerous relatives.

"Grandmamma, the man that we called on today in the village, addressed me by my name. How did he know who I was?"

"He knew my name too. Don't you remember Eliza? He said he was Uncle Samuel."

"But Grandfather called him something different, Risbee, I think it was."

"There was another Uncle too. His house was down by the water. He had a swing in his garden and there were lots of children to play with."

"That would be Mr William Nunn of Nether Hall, your grandfather's brother." The children were quite confused by the profusion of relatives. The girls also noticed a few differences between the farmers and those they had associated with in the city.

"The people speak strangely here." Mary's comment raised her grandmother's eyebrows a little.

"We pronounce certain words differently from Londoners here in the country, that's all Mary. You must get accustomed to that."

Another summer day's outing included a visit to Mistley Hall, the mansion that overlooked the village. "We called at the grand house on the hill today. Grandfather went inside. He had business to attend. We had to stay in the carriage."

"Thomas was that wise to take the girls there?" Mary Nunn spoke first to her husband, and then turned to her granddaughters with a serious look on her face. "The man who owns that house is a very important man. Now young ladies, you must always exhibit perfect behaviour if you should see him. There must never be any chattering, or squabbling, in his presence. Do you hear me? You must be especially mindful of your manners if you meet any of Mr Rigby's family. Please do not speak until you are spoken to and always use your deepest curtsy when you are addressed by such as them."

The Rigby's had been the major landholders in the Tendring Hundred for many years. When Richard Rigby inherited the Mistley Estate early in the eighteenth century he channelled his resources into building an industrial village there, complete with a port, ship yard, and malt-houses. He had the Mistley Thorn Inn built in 1724. It was designed as a staging post between London and Harwich for the comfort of travellers to the continent. He also built some terraced houses for the family's employees. The construction of a village church for Mistley began in 1730.

4 The Gentlemen Farmers

Richard Rigby's son continued his father's project in his time, gradually acquiring more and more land. He engaged Robert Adam to make architectural improvements to Mistley in the 1770's. The swan fountain was installed by Adam opposite the Mistley Thorn Inn as part of the project and two towers were added to the church. These became the structures that gave the village of Mistley its distinctive appearance.

Thomas Nunn (sen.) began his farming life as his father had done. They were Rigby's tenants. When his sons were born he held Bradfield Lodge. He inherited a further property in Wix from his father in 1782.[2] Then he became a leasehold tenant to the Rigby's at Little Bromley during the time that his sons, Thomas and Carrington, were growing up.[3] This property came into his hands through an inheritance of his wife Mary (née Carrington).

At the turn of the nineteenth century, controversy over Rigby's affairs resulted in large amounts of their property being sold off. Thomas Nunn (sen.) acquired his Lawford property at that time. His four brothers were also in a position to benefit and increase the Nunn family's holdings at the time of the Rigby sale.[4]

Old Thomas explained the history of the region to his grandchildren as they grew up. They learned to love the little hamlets and they could soon identify all their relatives. Mistley Village was special. The picturesque church towers and the swan fountain became important features in Eliza's childhood. She loved that graceful swan in its rippling blue pond, just as she enjoyed feeding the real swans that gathered by the malting buildings.

Carrington told Tom stories of his growing up years in the country. Tom's sisters often heard them second hand. The tales were mostly of fox chases. Mary thought that charging through fields and brambles after foxes was a dangerous and dirty way of having fun. Eliza thought it sounded exhilarating.

The family's involvement in the home defence of England intrigued Tom but it was something which caused Eliza to sigh loudly and dramatically whenever the subject was broached. The

4 The Gentlemen Farmers

Troop of Tendring Cavalry was quite a family affair. It included young Carrington and his father as well as Benjamin Carrington and Samuel Risbee, his uncles.

"Tell me about your cavalry, Uncle."

"We formed up at the time of the French Revolution, in 1793. We called ourselves the Tendring Loyal Volunteers."

"It sounds rather a laugh."

"We were quite in earnest, I can assure you, young man. Even now, an invasion by Napoléon remains a threat here on the coast. We met together to practise manoeuvres and tactics in case of an attack. Your grandfather stood as the Lieutenant of the force. He drilled us regularly under Captain John Hanson of Great Bromley Hall.[5] Oh yes, we gentrified farmers took our defence role very seriously. We had order books printed and our own colours."[6]

"Was that the flag I saw in Grandfather's study? He said it belonged to his cavalry. But I hadn't heard he went to war, did he?"

"No, we've been spared any trouble so far down here on home territory. Would you like to hear our special song?"

"How does that go? Do sing it, do!" Uncle Carrington was very happy to boom out the lines of the cavalry's song.

> *Ye volunteers all, Who honour the call of your King and your old Constitution. Supporting the cause of Religion and Laws, Severed at the Great Revolution...*[7]

In addition to the gentlemen's cavalry, Essex was under the protection of the local militia. During the war years, every adult male in England was liable to serve in the county militia. Conscription for this was by ballot.

Thomas Nunn (sen.) was appointed a Deputy Lieutenant by the Lord Lieutenant of the Essex Militia in 1801. He was a magistrate by then so he was not required to serve in the regiment but it was his task to oversee the conscription lists and balloting. Carrington became a Deputy Lieutenant in 1809.[8] This was a prestigious civic appointment that signified a gentleman's position in the community as someone of consequence.[9]

4 The Gentlemen Farmers

John Hanson and Thomas Nunn (sen.) were close friends.[10] Not only did they run the cavalry together. They also established the East Essex Hunts in 1798. The gentlemen horsemen of the Tendring Hundred met together for foxhunting once the fields lay fallow after the harvest. From November to March, they would meet at least twice a week to participate in the chase. Hanson, together with the Hanbury family of Coggeshall, managed the hounds in those early days.

Thomas Nunn (jun.) and his brother Carrington were introduced to the hunt as soon as they donned breeches. They both became skilled participants and established a name for themselves in the sport as young men.[11] When John Hanson moved from the area, the hounds were transferred to the Nunn's farm. Carrington took over their care. The Nunn family organised the East Essex Hunt for many decades after that.

The cost of purchasing and maintaining suitable hunters did not come cheaply. The equipment required, as well as the costs of keeping a groom, made foxhunting prohibitive for those without the means.

Young Tom inevitably followed his father and uncle into such outdoor pursuits. The young man enjoyed far greater liberty than his sisters.

In winter particularly, girls were kept confined to the house. They were not permitted to join the hunt. Eliza and Mary were allowed to watch the men gather at the start of a day's sport. Sometimes Uncle Carrington might even lift them up onto his huge beast for a time as he described the day's course to his friends, but the girls were not encouraged to linger amongst the commotion for long. Grandmother Nunn would soon fetch them inside on those cold frosty mornings, hurrying them out of the way of horses, dogs and burly men.

Fox hunting was a male-dominated sport. The necessity of using a side-saddle prevented women participating in the galloping and dare devil jumping required to keep up the chase.

4 The Gentlemen Farmers

Hearing of their brother's escapades and adventures became a cause of frustration for Mary and Eliza as they approached adolescence. Yet the Nunn girls were more privileged than many other young ladies. Thomas Nunn, being such an ardent equestrian, held that it was important for his daughters to ride well – with restrictions. Not only were they limited to using a side-saddle, they were also forbidden to ride without a groom to lead them. Their rides were always taken at a gentle walking pace.

However much they longed to thunder over open fields with their hair whipping out of place and the rising dust covering their riding habits, such exploits were not to be for Tom's sisters. Once they proved themselves young women of decorum and common sense, they were allowed a little freedom on their steeds, but the pace was always sedate and they were never to be far from their groom or their father.

Females were not completely excluded from the hunt gatherings though. Later, as grown women, they would be permitted to attend the hunt as observers. Naturally, attendance at the hunt balls was mandatory for Thomas Nunn's daughters as it was for all the elite young women of the county.

6 The Hunt Ball, John Leech

5 The Londoners

Despite the sheltered existence they led, the two sisters were fortunate in other ways. They enjoyed the company of an enormous extended family in Essex. They also had a London family whom they visited occasionally during the festive season.

Sarah Nicholson still lived in the huge house on Loam Pit Hill. It made a magnificent place for family Christmas gatherings. Those were the high days of Eliza's childhood.

Unlike their quiet country home, the noise at Stone House was tremendous, with a cacophony of children's squeals and squabbles. For Eliza it was a relief to be allowed to have fun.

The Nicholson clan had grown substantially by the end of 1813. Ann's other sisters and her brother, Frederick, were all married with children.[1] Louisa, the youngest, was married at sixteen to the son of the builder to whom Frederick had been apprenticed – William Rolfe was an architect.

Eliza had city cousins of all ages. Together they made a great noisy horde. Ann Dowley, daughter of Aunt Sarah, was almost exactly the same age as Eliza. Cousin Harriot was just a few months younger. Tom enjoyed the company of Uncle Frederick's boys: Fred and Harry were ten and eleven. The three of them loved to tease and taunt the younger girls.

Uncle Frederick and Aunt Elizabeth had three smaller children too – little Elizabeth, Alfred, and Emma. James and Charles were the sons of Aunt Harriot and Thomas Dowley, with their little sister Maria. Then there were the babies, Fanny, Margaret and William.

Amelia and Edward Creasy, named for their parents, lived near Deptford too.

The rich aroma of a roasted goose filled the house and the squeals of overexcited children penetrated every room. Compared to Mary, Sarah was an indulgent and tolerant grandmother. She always seemed to have treats tucked away in the pockets of her skirts. There were scattered toys everywhere, dolls and tin soldiers, tops and skittles, building blocks and fabric balls all strategically placed to trip up any maid moving too fast through her tasks.

The cousins were put to service for days before the event, cutting and folding streamers to hang around the walls, and festooning the staircase with evergreens. Loud renditions of carols echoed through the vast house. They took turns at the pianoforte, showing off their various skills 'with extreme onction [sic] (playing) upon the pianoforte, harp, guitar, triangle and castagnettes [sic] with all (their) might, all singing at once.'[2]

On Christmas morning, the family coaches set off down the hill for church, crunching through freshly fallen snow, beckoned on by bells pealing joyfully in the distance. The Church of St Paul's in Deptford was a splendid structure with plenty to capture childish imaginations. In spite of the restrictions placed on their behaviour in church, all the cousins looked forward to the outing.

Sarah's grandchildren scrambled noisily up the steps together, entering into the breath-taking space through the large double doors. Inside, glittering chandeliers hung from gilt chains, twinkling and sparkling above the heads of the worshippers. Towering columns lined the aisles. The stout posts supported ornate balconies that jutted out above the main gallery.

Eliza adored singing Christmas carols. In church, she held her hymn book high, imitating the choristers. She sang loudly and lustily, endeavouring to hear herself above the rest of the congregation and the organ.

"Shush, don't sing so loud," her cousin poked her.

"Why not? Everyone else is." Eliza prodded her back.

5 The Londoners

"Children aren't supposed to sing!"
"We sing in Mistley, I love singing."
"You are so countrified Eliza."
"Please try to behave with a little more decorum, children."

Aunt Harriot looked down on them with a frown of disapproval. The censure diminished Eliza's delight in the visit and was not something she was quick to forget.

7 St Paul's Church Deptford, used with permission of Lewisham Local History and Archives Centre

Another occasion was etched in Eliza's memory also. After the Christmas celebrations of 1813 had finished, temperatures across the country plummeted to record lows. A dense fog settled. Those who had ventured to London for the holiday season were stranded. The frost bit hard and the heaviest snowfall in centuries followed.

51

5 The Londoners

A slight thaw at the beginning of the New Year allowed some temporary respite from the cold but in London, the ice on the Thames broke into chunks that jammed between the bridges, effectively damming the river.

By the end of the month the Thames between Blackfriars Bridge and London Bridge was a solid surface of ice. Rather than losing the meagre incomes they depended on, resourceful vendors soon set up stalls on the frozen river.

Thomas Nunn, held up longer than he had expected to be in London, decided to take his son to the Frost Fair. His brothers-in-law had suggested a family outing. Although Thomas was reluctant to allow his delicate daughters to be mixed up in an unsavoury crowd, that did not prevent the little girls from beseeching him.

"Father, do take us too, please, please?" Since some of their cousins were going, Thomas relented. "Only for a short time mind, and you must not let go of my hand."

Everyone who was able ventured out to enjoy the spectacle. The aristocracy attended, as well as the ordinary folk of the city. There were ragged urchins, over-sized matrons wrapped in their shawls, strutting young men in tight-fitting buckskins and old, unshaved men in battered hats. Such a mob proved to be a frighteningly overwhelming experience for children now better used to peaceful rural vistas. The girls were obedient, and stayed close to their father, feeling safe in his protection.

Food, toys, books and all manner of wares were for sale across the expanse of the river dubbed Freeze-land Street. There were skittle alleys and a skating rink too. To demonstrate the thickness of the ice some daring characters led an elephant across the river beneath Blackfriars Bridge.

Four days later, the tide shifted the mass of ice, allowing the river water to flow freely once more. That caused a swift close to the fair.

Tom attended Charterhouse School in London later in the year of 1814. Charterhouse was a small elite school for educating the sons of gentry. He made friends at that school. One of them was

5 The Londoners

John Ayles, a young man he was later to get to know more intimately.

8 Charterhouse School 1805

The Peace Celebrations that the Regent provided for the public's entertainment, in August 1814, were spectacular. After being at war for more than twenty years, the nation was celebrating Napoléon's imprisonment on the island of Elba. Being in London for the events, Tom and his schoolmates had permission to attend. They enjoyed the re-enactment of Nelson's victory on the Serpentine and the fireworks in Hyde Park.

The seemingly endless stories of war had caught the imagination of every young lad in the country. Two of Tom's schoolmates had an older cousin who was an officer in the Royal Marines. He was off fighting in America. The boys strutted up and down the playground pretending to be soldiers like the Lieutenant.

"Men, take your arms. Load. Take aim. Fire!" Tom called the drill.

It was from her brother that Eliza first heard the name, Lieutenant Lewis Agassiz, mentioned.

That same year, Thomas Nunn (jun.) was appointed a Deputy Lieutenant for the Essex Militia.[3] He also joined his father in the banking industry.[4] He was thirty-seven years old. With the new partnership in place, he secured two buildings in Manningtree to function as the bank premises.

Thomas Nunn (jun.) swore his oath of allegiance to the Crown as a Justice of the Peace in the Tendring Hundred in April 1816. He resigned his seat on the Brewers' Court later that year bringing his London brewing ventures to a close.[5] Thomas had maintained his position on the Court for the six years that had passed since he left London even though he no longer attended the meetings.

6 The Village Gossip

"I heard something about our neighbour's son today, Thomas," Grandmother Nunn was probing her husband for information. She was hoping old Thomas would know more about the rumours she had heard in the village.

"Mrs Nunn, you've been gossiping again haven't you?" Her husband scolded. "I wish you wouldn't listen to hearsay."

The elderly woman ignored his remonstrance and continued. "Young George Bridges has been up to mischief. I always knew he was a spoiled young man, such a disgrace to his family. Now he's ruined a young woman's reputation. I really can't believe it, and him a man of the cloth!"

"Who are you talking about Grandmamma?" Overhearing the conversation, Eliza was inquisitive.

"George Wilson Bridges, the eldest son of Lawford Place yonder, not that you should be listening."

"The handsome one you mean? I remember him at that ball you took us to there, years ago now. You let us watch from the balcony when Master George and Miss Godfrey took the opening dance.[1]

"So I did, you lucky girl. It's very impolite to eavesdrop on adults Eliza, you should know better now you're ten."

"They made an elegant couple Grandmamma; do you think they will be married?"

"No, that pair'll not be wed. Off you go now and mind your own business."

Eliza obediently skipped off and Thomas returned to his newspaper. However, Mary had not finished. She dropped her voice and continued to speak.

6 The Village Gossip

"He's eloped to Scotland you know Thomas. I do so feel for his mother." Thomas realised with resignation that he was not going to escape the conversation after all.

"Ah yes, that's what took our neighbour George to London last week. I thought he was having business trouble. He told me today that it was to see the couple properly wed and settled. The young Reverend has been given an appointment in Jamaica. Best to keep them out of the way of the scandalmongers for a while, the family thought."[2]

"Well you could have told me if you knew already Thomas!"

"I didn't think it was a story worth repeating Mary. There's been enough shame for the family without it becoming common gossip." Soon after that Eliza's grandparents had new neighbours, for the Bridges sold their home and moved back to London.[3]

Napoléon was imprisoned once more, and the war with America resolved by 1816. Despite that, the end of hostilities abroad brought little change to the quiet Stour Valley.

Being such a close community, there were plenty of tales to be heard and remarked upon. Eliza and Mary aged ten and twelve might have eavesdropped on the talk of the grownups but they were too young to understand the full implications of the conversations they overheard.

It was inevitable that, when the attention paid to the Widow Phillebrown by a particular young gentleman was noticed, it would set the village mouths to work. Mary Nunn was not so happy to listen to that tale. Agassiz, a young marine, was on leave from the Woolwich barracks. He was visiting a fellow officer in the locality.[4]

Young Tom, who now attended the grammar school in Dedham, recognised the name when he heard the story mentioned at school and brought it up with his father.

"I've heard of Lewis Agassiz. Some lads I knew from Charterhouse claimed him as cousin. He was a Lieutenant in the Royal Marines back then, off fighting in America. They told us some remarkable accounts of his adventures." Eleven-year-old Tom's voice was full of admiration for the valiant soldier.

9 Lady Wanton's Reputation in Danger, George Cruikshank

6 The Village Gossip

"Father do you think we might get to meet Agassiz sometime? I've heard ever so many stories about him. He's quite the hero you know."

Tom's father was not sure about that, he disapproved of the talk he had heard connecting the marine with his cousin, Elizabeth. Elegant and accomplished, Elizabeth was beautiful – and rich. The Nunn's suspected this Agassiz was a fortune hunter.

The gossip that Thomas had heard of his cousin was correct. It was clear to all that Lieutenant Lewis Agassiz was enamoured with Mrs Elizabeth Phillebrown. The only daughter of Robert Nunn was equally smitten and encouraged the young man's devotion.[5] The small community frowned upon such open admiration and preferential behaviour. Though the gossips did allow for this being a love match, they were quick to note that the heiress was an extremely fortunate catch for the twenty-three year old officer.

The rumours were quashed when Lewis married Elizabeth a respectable year and three days after the death of her husband. Thomas's Uncle Robert gave a public blessing to the marriage then. He was pleased his only daughter had found happiness at last. For her, after a childless marriage, Agassiz was a chance at a new start in life. She was still young, albeit thirteen years older than her new husband.

The couple moved out of the way of the gossips of Mistley, settling much closer to London in Loughton. Further talk would have been excited had the neighbourhood known how shortly after their marriage Elizabeth had given birth to their first child.

By 1819, Eliza's Grandmother Nunn was starting to fail and could no longer manage both of her son's households as well as her own. At his mother's prompting, Thomas finally wed again.

His new wife was Mrs Marianne Ayles of Woodford Cottage, Leyton, in West Essex. Marianne, née Mount was a Londoner like Thomas's first wife. She was the widow of John Ayles, a shipbuilder of Wapping. By her previous marriage, she had one son, John, who turned sixteen the year she married Thomas.[6] Eliza, Mary and Tom were of a similar age to their new stepbrother, John.

6 The Village Gossip

Mary Nunn died the following year.[7] Old Sarah Nicholson had passed away too.[8]

A new wife for their father meant changes in Eliza's life. Marianne was a sociable, lively woman. She enjoyed company. That brought more variety to all their lives. Before long Marianne and Thomas added to their combined family. Two little girls, Matilda and Henrietta were born.[9] Eliza and Mary took great delight in playing with their baby sisters. To them they were like living dolls.

At first Marianne was worried that living in the remote valley would be boring but she soon found that life for the genteel inhabitants of the Stour Valley involved the same circuit of polite gatherings and social events that she was used to in London. There were dinner parties and card evenings. Private balls were regularly held at Mistley Hall. Good assemblies were held in Dedham throughout the year as well as the splendid garrison balls and entertaining theatre productions based in Colchester. She was often called on to be hostess at numerous hunt balls herself.

In summer, the families of the area met for picnics and mounted excursions to nearby beaches.[10] Fossil-hunting expeditions to the beach at Walton-on-the-Naze were particularly enjoyed by young and old.

The Agassiz family, Lewis, Elizabeth and their little daughter, returned to the valley in 1823. Their notoriety had long since been forgotten. The couple became frequent visitors to the Nunn's lively home. Marianne and Elizabeth developed a close friendship. The two women were a similar age and both knew what it was to be widowed. Elizabeth's daughter was just a little older than Marianne's two. Elizabeth was invaluable support to Marianne when she was grieving her infant son's death.[11] Elizabeth knew what it was to lose a son.[12]

Marianne, as with the other ladies of the area, spent at least one afternoon a week addressing cards for her friends. These were formal invitations to attend her 'At Home' afternoons. The women sipped tea from delicate painted china and consumed dainty morsels, seated around a pretty, cloth-covered table.

6 The Village Gossip

Busy as they were nurturing their offspring and managing servants, the women enjoyed whispering over their husbands' quirks and eccentricities. They shared child-rearing problems, favourite novels and embroidery patterns.

While the women chattered, Eliza and Mary supervised games amongst the younger children. They were used to caring for their half-sisters so Elizabeth Agassiz was glad to entrust her little daughter to the young women's care whenever she visited her friend.

On one such afternoon, the ladies were seated on the lawn watching their children play. As Marianne handed her friend a brimming cup of tea, she could not resist addressing the subject that was on her mind.

"I heard you and Mr Agassiz caused quite a stir in the village once."

"Oh that was years ago!" Elizabeth laughed.

"It was true then? You had an affair?"

"Is that what they say? I suppose, since I was a widow, we had more freedom than most lovers. You could say we made use of the situation." That comment set the company off in titters.

"Lewis was so transparently single-minded when he met me," Elizabeth recalled. "He was torn between returning to his regiment and staying on in Mistley, but I won over the call to attend the troops, many times. He was a romantic, still is, the dear boy! The other ladies were quite envious of Elizabeth with her devoted, dashing young husband.

"Thomas was more reserved. I was never quite sure that he was in love with me. But then he went into an absolute panic when I was expecting Matilda. I enjoyed the fuss he made. Oh dear, I mustn't discuss things like that in front of his girls." Childbirth stories were kept to a discreet level. Even amongst women that was a barely acceptable subject.

If gossip was in short supply then apparel inevitably became the topic of choice. Bonnets, gloves, and parasols were discussed at length amongst the ladies. By that time fashions were changing. The high-waisted muslins of the Regency were no longer in vogue. Fitted bodices and full skirts that enhanced the natural waistline rather than the high-busted silhouette of previous years replaced them. Mary and Eliza were allowed to be party to such conversations.

It was at the end of the summer, in 1824, that Mary married John, Marianne's son by her previous marriage.[13]

For Eliza, performing the duties of bridesmaid at her sister's wedding marked small alteration in her already quiet existence. If anything, her life became a little more subdued. She missed her elder sister's constant chatter. The harmless bickering in which they had occasionally engaged became something she remembered with nostalgia. Caring for her younger siblings developed into the principal occupation for the young woman.

When the arrival of winter heralded the close of 1825, everyone knew that Elizabeth Agassiz was poorly: she was too unwell to visit her neighbours or to attend the parties. Marianne sent her husband to call for news.

"I'm glad you're home, dear. I'm so anxious to hear. How is Elizabeth faring?" Marianne greeted her husband with some agitation on his return.

"There's no good news. Agassiz is trying to keep a stoical good humour but I can see his desolation. He told me that Elizabeth could not even raise her head from the pillow yesterday. I can't imagine he's good in the sick room," Thomas reported to his wife.

A few days later, Marianne and Eliza called at Stour Lodge themselves to leave their cards and enquire after their friend. They returned with the six-year-old Elizabeth Mary Ann, thinking it best she stayed with them while there was sickness in the house.

Elizabeth died just three days after Christmas.[14] Her grief-stricken husband shut himself away, unable to face the world for a time. His little girl remained with the Nunn family, but she was miserable, quite lost and confused, without her parents.

Eliza, nearly twenty years of age, was pleased to take the role of nurturing the forlorn child. She proved herself a devoted and protective carer with an innate understanding of how the motherless child felt.

6 The Village Gossip

Through January, and February, little Elizabeth Agassiz stayed on in the household. Eliza was so busy with the infants that she ceased to miss her sister. Winter turned to spring, bringing the welcome signs of summer. Eliza oversaw the children's reading and writing lessons in the nursery during the mornings, and then took them out to the garden as the weather improved.

Balmy afternoons were spent outdoors in summer bonnets. There were squeals of laughter as the youngsters took turns on the swing, played tag with the dog and practised with their hoops. The groom even brought round the dog cart on occasion for them to play at driving.

Lewis Agassiz began to appear, quietly standing on the edge of the garden, just watching. A little thinner and paler, he was gradually emerging from mourning. Occasionally he would smile at the antics.

"Papa, come and play!" His daughter was thrilled to see him.

"Yes please do, Mr Agassiz, for the child's sake," Eliza added.

Responding to his daughter's enthusiasm Lewis began self-consciously joining in with the girl-games. It was not long before the widower forgot to feel awkward and instead found he was enjoying himself. The healing process was underway.

Eliza could see how Elizabeth blossomed as her father recovered. He soon had the girls shrieking and clapping their hands with glee as he chased them around the paths and caught them, swinging them into the air, petticoats flying. "Me too, me too!" was the catch cry that summer. It was unusual for little girls to enjoy such attention from an adult male.

Lewis had hardly noticed Eliza before that time. She had only recently been allowed to attend adult entertainments. In those situations his wife eclipsed every other woman present.

The pair became better acquainted during the summer as they minded the girls together. They were in a unique position to develop a relationship. Theirs became a friendship that might have been considered by some to be closer than was regular.

"Come on girls, let's go for a walk!" Lewis suggested one afternoon. "Summer will be drawing to a close soon."

62

He and Eliza had been watching the antics from beneath the shade of a tree. He took her by the arm and off they all went. They walked down the hill towards Mistley's church, and then along the Wall to feed the stately mute swans that gathered there.

With the sun low in the sky behind them, the estuary glowed, reflecting the warmth of the day. Out across the mud at the water's edge, flocks of plovers, pintails and knots sparkled in the distance. It was a pleasing, restful scene with a hint of magic in the air.

Eliza and Lewis admired the beauty together. Their arms remained linked, perhaps a little longer than was necessary.

Eliza was composing a painting in her mind, quite absorbed with the scene, but Lewis's thoughts were directed in a different direction.

He quietly took note of the gentle girl on his arm. Despite her youth, he had developed a great respect for her over the summer. Sensible, caring, but not altogether biddable, she had proven herself reliable and intelligent. Above all he was aware of the close bond that had developed between Eliza and his daughter. Lewis did not want to risk disrupting that connection. He knew his friend Thomas would provide Eliza with a worthwhile settlement.

The young woman had dreams of her own. What she wanted was to escape the confines of her country life. Lewis knew that. She told him that she wanted to establish her own home – a house that would be full of fun and noise and mad adventures, so different from the quiet, controlled childhood she had experienced. They talked of her desire to live in the city and to travel, over those summer afternoons in the garden.

As autumn progressed, Lewis took his group of damsels on more outings. Whenever the weather allowed he took the girls walking. They gathered mushrooms from the fields and then chestnuts from the woods behind their home.

Lewis appreciated the sentiment of Eliza's dreams. He wanted to escape too, to be free of sorrowful memories. It was time to move on. Lewis was ready to face new challenges.

However, he must survive Christmas before that could happen.

10 Feeding the Swans

7 The Lovers

Icicles hung from the bare trees and there was a thick carpet of snow on the ground. The Christmas of 1826 was more than typically cold and frosty. It was cold enough for great lumps of ice to have been seen floating in the Thames. The newspaper reports of such gave London folk reason to wonder whether there would be another frost fair that year.[1]

The short hours of daylight, the bitter cold and boggy roads all conspired to limit society and confine gentlefolk like the Nunn family to their homes. Nevertheless, the small, close-knit communities near Mistley made the most of the short holiday period.

It was certainly a time for family gatherings, carols and warm hearths. Houses were filled with decorations and the spicy scent of simmering plum puddings. There were parties, private dances and informal concerts to attend. Adolescent sons came home from school and married daughters visited their aging parents with their young broods.

Thomas Nunn's household was preparing for visitors.[2] Their large home in Mistley was going to be overflowing that Christmas. Lewis Agassiz and his little daughter might stay for a few days. Grandfather Nunn, living alone in Lawford House, a short distance away, had been persuaded to venture out but he would remain only for a night or two, he preferred his own bed. The widow of Grandfather's brother Henry, Mary, would accompany him and so would Carrington.

Sarah Eliza Nunn prepared for the festive season as she had for every year that she could remember. She industriously worked small

7 The Lovers

gifts for her family by hand: daintily edged handkerchiefs for her stepmother and a muffler for her father. For her sister, Eliza planned to crochet a shawl of finest spun wool. She used scraps of fabric to clothe the two china dolls her father had bought for his younger daughters.

Some days, if it was too dark to stitch, she ventured into the kitchen to help Cook prepare the pastries, gingerbread and other treats that would be needed with the house expected to be so full. The kitchen was the warmest room in the house and cook was always happy to have an extra pair of hands to help – as long as she did as she was told. The currant cakes were long since done, having been set aside to mature at the end of autumn.

Mary and John arrived a week before the celebrations began. Thomas's eyebrows rose when he saw the quantity of luggage they brought.

"Those are weighty trunks coming in Mary. How long are you expecting to stay?" They were clearly planning to stay for a while.

"You can be sure we're here for Christmas dear Father, I hope you are pleased. Beaumont is so cold."

Thomas recalled that his wife had once complained that Mary had a tendency to be most concerned with her own comfort and was sometimes oblivious to other people's feelings. At the time Thomas had ignored such comments as he was aware of the difficulties Marianne faced with the care of his older children. Perhaps she was right.

"Do you know it was below freezing point in the house all week? Mr Ayles refuses to pay for a fire in my chamber so the wash water has been frozen every day. I don't know how long we will be staying, but at least until there are signs of a thaw. You don't mind do you Papa dear?"

Eliza was pleased to see her sister. She still missed Mary, though she only lived a short drive away, and looked forward to spending time with her. As they had always done when they were children, the sisters set about decorating the house together. They had an array of sweetly fragrant evergreens brought in by the groom.

7 The Lovers

In high spirits, Eliza and Mary draped holly and ivy, rosemary and laurel in artistic swathes over the mantels above the roaring fires. The branches brightened the outlook and refreshed the fusty air of a house kept tightly closed against the winter chill. Coloured paper decorations took them hours to fashion before they too were hung about the reception rooms. They played duets on the pianoforte in the evenings and whispered girl's talk over their needlework.

"Eliza, it's time for a chat," began her sister one evening. "Marianne tells me that you've been getting to know Mr Agassiz of late. It seems you've been spending a great deal of time with him."

"You know I've had the care of his daughter for this past year. We've enjoyed a few strolls together – mainly in Father's garden, while I mind the girls."

"And is he as elegant and informed as they say?"

"Well he is interesting Mary. I feel quite at ease with him."

"Your sense of ease hasn't led to any impropriety I hope Sister."

"Of course not Mary, he's far too respectable for unseemly behaviour. Besides, he misses our Cousin Elizabeth tremendously. When he's not brooding over her, he's totally absorbed by his daughter."

"He makes a rather handsome widower I imagine?" Eliza blushed at her sister's tone.

"I don't think he's even aware of me Mary. Elizabeth was so beautiful and he really did love her."

"He certainly profited well by such a love match then!"

"You'd have more respect for him if you knew him better Mary."

Their father had already visited Lewis Agassiz with an invitation, under instructions from his wife again.

"You must make sure Mr Agassiz promises to be here for Christmas Thomas. Eliza thinks it best to keep little Elizabeth occupied with familiar company and friends her own age – and it would be beneficial for him too. I think Christmas is a good time for a widower to begin again, however hard that might be for him." Just approaching the end of first mourning as Lewis was, it was seemly for the man to begin participating in social engagements.

7 The Lovers

"I must admit I'm not looking forward to Christmas. It seems rather a hurdle to be survived," Lewis confessed to his friend.

"It's Elizabeth that concerns me. I know she has managed the year quite well, considering all and thanks in no small amount to your family's hospitality. Your daughter Eliza's care has been really beneficial to her. But Christmas will be hard on us. I'm not looking forward to it at all." Lewis cupped his glass of port in two hands and stared dejectedly at the carpet.

"Well then, my friend, I have a suggestion." Thomas understood what his friend was suffering. He did not need to pause to consider the invitation he had come to deliver. "There is no doubt about it; you must both spend the festive season with us! I am sure my girls will all be thrilled." Truly they were.

The night before Christmas, Marianne Nunn secretly devised a hanging decoration of mistletoe arranged with pine cones and silk bows above the entrance to the drawing room. When Marianne revealed her surprise arrangement to her husband, he grimaced at her mischievousness.

"Oh I know," she admitted, "It's a little unrefined, something usually reserved for the servant's quarters, but I want to add some sparkle to the occasion, to lighten the atmosphere. Mr Agassiz has been so morose and serious this past year – a bit of merriment might be the prompt he needs. You know what I mean," she added with a twinkle in her eye that only made her husband groan further.

"What are you up to Marianne? I can see you're hatching a plan. Why do women have to interfere and meddle?"

"Thomas, that's unfair!"

"I know dear, however silly it all sounds to an old fellow like me," he was fatalistic about letting her have her way, "you have the family's best interests at heart."

"I'm quite determined that we shall all have a jolly time and enjoy the season. You know that's all I want. Last Christmas was so miserable," she added. Marianne was also looking forward to a time when Thomas's older children would no longer be her responsibility but she would never admit that to anyone.

11 Some Christmas Faces, Illustrated Times

The bells of St Mary's Church pealed with joy as Christmas Day dawned. Together the family, and their visitors, braved softly falling snow to walk down the road for the morning's service. Later, after the carols, a stern sermon and many good wishes from their neighbours, they returned home to enjoy the roaring fire.

"Off you go Elizabeth, wish your friends a Merry Christmas." Shyly, with much prompting and whispering from her father, the little girl presented her friends with the latest children's books, 'Grimm's Fairy Tales' for Matilda and a copy of the recently published American poem, 'The Night before Christmas' for Hetty. Eliza sat down to read the new volumes aloud to the children.'

Then when the little ones could no longer keep still, Eliza occupied them with games. 'Hunt the Slipper' and 'Hood Man Blind' kept the youngsters amused for the rest of the afternoon. The gentlemen reclined with their port while Marianne and Mary vanished for a rest.

The gong sounded. It reminded the family to retire to dress for dinner. Their nurse whisked off the children and Eliza was alone with her maid. She had a new gown to wear that evening. A gift from her parents, it was yellow, shimmery and bright. She stood in front of the looking glass, enjoying the swish of silk, pleased with what she saw. Her fair hair was caught back in a knot, braided loops hanging about her ears, with a little holly entwined in the chignon.

"There," said her maid, with a final pat to Eliza's hair. You be lookin' beau'ful now Miss. You'll attract the gen'leman's note this ev'nin' to be sure."

"Whatever do you mean? I'm not sure I want to attract anyone's notice," replied Eliza rather diffidently.

Nevertheless, Eliza's cheeks were flushed and her eyes bright when they assembled in the drawing room. Her father greeted her with a nod and a peck on the cheek.

"Not too overdone Father?" she asked.

"You look dazzling my dear," he replied. It was his responsibility to make his daughters feel beautiful.

"Quite the Belle," agreed Mr Agassiz who was waiting to escort his hostess downstairs into dinner. That comment raised the flush on Eliza's cheeks even more so. It was not really his place to make such an observation.

12 Dinner Dress 1826, Ackermann's Repository of Arts

    Marianne soon entered the room, ready to lead the family to the table on Lewis's arm. Mary, next in precedence with her father, followed them into the dining room. Grandfather and the widow

7 The Lovers

trailed behind, leaving John Ayles to escort Eliza. The order was strategic for it seated Eliza next to Lewis at the table.

That evening, the entire company celebrated the season in high spirits, stoked by convivial games and glasses of fizzing champagne. They played 'Snap Dragon' with great uproar, snatching raisins and almonds from a flaming bowl of brandy. Everyone agreed that the most entertaining occurrence of their Christmas party was when they played 'Bullet Pudding'.

Lewis took his turn at slicing the heaped up flour pudding with the knife.

"Oh no! I didn't do that at all well, there it goes!" Everyone laughed as the bullet toppled off the pile into the white dust below.

"Well, I'd better get it over and obey the rules," he announced gallantly, and plunged his chin into the choking powder, holding his breath as he sought the bullet. Seconds later he triumphantly emerged with it between his teeth. Claps of delight greeted his ghostly grin.

Sarah Eliza was feeling quite deliciously giddy, when Lewis, in a surprisingly jovial manner, whisked her off to the mistletoe and kissed her before she realised what was happening!

"Oh, Mr Agassiz! What would Father say?" She did so hope no one had noticed. But her step-mother smiled and caught her husband's eye. Warmth, laughter, plenty of delectable treats and fine company had made for a lovely day.

The following day was St Stephen's Day. The ladies set off to visit around the village, taking apples and homemade cider as gifts while Lewis disappeared with Thomas into the study. This was not an unusual occurrence – the men often had business to discuss, but Eliza was a little perplexed. She thought such matters could have been postponed until after the festival.

Then the holiday was over. Little Elizabeth was all smiles as she embraced her friends and said goodbye. She and her father climbed aboard Lewis's carriage and departed for their own home the next day. Lewis was not planning to participate in the seasonal field sports that year.

7 The Lovers

28 December, Holy Innocents Day, was to be a quiet day of remembrance for the two of them.

New Year's Eve and the days that followed were quieter days for the women of the Nunn household too. The menfolk, Thomas Nunn, his father, his son and his brother Carrington were inevitably led by the horn and galloped off fox hunting with John Ayles and most of the other gentlemen of the neighbourhood.

Though busy with the children as ever, Eliza was distracted by memories of mistletoe. She knew Mr Agassiz well enough to know that he did nothing without careful consideration. Twelfth night was looming, a celebratory cake and an evening dance at Mistley Hall meant that she was looking forward to the possibility of seeing him once more. Romance was on her mind.

Marianne encouraged her stepdaughters to read some of the ladies' publications that she ordered by post from the Capital. This was to check the newest London styles and embroidery designs, but they both enjoyed peeking through the romance stories too.

"You're unusually quiet these days Eliza. Are you feeling well?"

"Quite well Mary, just thinking. Have you read the latest issue of Marianne's quarterly?"

"There's a nice ball dress design in there."

"And a lovely serial story, very romantic."

"Eliza, what would Grandmother say if she knew you were reading those?" Mary scolded with a smile on her face, then she continued. "But I know the one you mean, with the handsome Fredrico."

"Hmm, he's a scoundrel!"

"But a charmer, I think. I loved the bit where he rescued the Countess and carried her off to his lair."

"He seized her hand and pressed it, in a transport of joy to his lips and to his heart."[5] Eliza knew the scene by heart.

"Why Eliza, you didn't even need to read it! That makes me suspicious that my little sister is in love! You can't hide it from me." Eliza blushed at that. She really had not wished to be so transparent.

"Don't tease Mary, please don't!"

7 The Lovers

Lewis did not disappoint when they finally met again. On the evening of 5 January 1827 Mr Agassiz was almost unrecognisably charming.

"Good evening Miss Nunn. May I request a reservation on your card?" He sought Eliza out as a dance partner soon after their arrival. In fact he failed to leave her side all evening. He brought her refreshments and was generally more attentive than any dreamy girl could have fancied.

A few flicks of fans from the matrons' corner caught Eliza's eye and she realised others had noticed his attention. "Oh bother the old ladies, I won't be embarrassed. I'm enjoying myself and I've nothing to blush about." That rebellious little thought gave her the confidence to enjoy his interest.

During the waltz he held her firmly, a little too close perhaps, Eliza was undecided. He was near enough for her to smell the combination of carbolic soap and Makassar oil, the usual ingredients of a male toilette. Lewis definitely had a sense of purpose that evening.

"That girl has allowed Mr Agassiz a sight too many turns around the floor."

"Have you noticed his waistcoat? It's rather overt for a widower just out of mourning I would have thought."

"Yes, he's strutting like a peacock in pursuit tonight."

"Well, he's certainly getting the encouragement to continue his quest."

"I'd have hoped the young lady could be more demure about her responses. What would Old Mary say if she saw her granddaughter behave in such a way? Marianne's not doing anything to prevent Sarah Eliza making a fool of herself, I notice."

Towards the close of the evening, the suitor drew Eliza aside to the library. No one was surprised and no one moved to interrupt them. If they had, Marianne was ready to intervene. Even though the situation was so transparently obvious, Lewis Agassiz still managed to startle Sarah Eliza Nunn with his formal proposal of marriage. He went down on his knees and declared endless devoted love.

13 The Proposal, John Leech

He had already discussed the idea with her father; they had gone so far as to agree the financial details at Christmas. However, her father would not force her into a marriage that could not make her happy. He would follow Eliza's preference. Choosing a husband was the most serious decision of a young woman's life, quite possibly the only important decision she would ever make for herself.

The dancing finished, the evening drew to a close and the coach delivered the family home.

"Do I really have a choice?" Eliza wondered aloud as her maid brushed out her hair in the early hours of the morning.

"You'd be thinkin' o' Mr Agassy Miss?"

"He's asked me to call him 'Lewis' but I can't help thinking of him as Mr Agassiz. He's so old."

"Not that old Miss. It be a good thing if a man be mature for then 'e's better off. Can'e provide for you Miss Eliza? D'you know 'is prospects? What's'e worth? Those be the 'portant fac's Miss."

"He does have a nice home," Eliza answered thoughtfully.

7 The Lovers

"It's rather small but it was Cousin Elizabeth's design and she clearly thought it was adequate. It's full of all her furniture, her pictures, her silverware. Could I make it my own?"

"P'raps a change of drapes'd help that Miss."

"As to what he's worth; that's a question for my father to satisfy. I don't think money matters if there is love."

"It'd be love then Miss?"

"That and the promise of a family, a home I can make my own – I don't want to be stuck here all my life. I want to see the world. I want to have fun!"

Eliza realised she had learned more about Lewis in the past few months, and she liked what she had discovered. He was kind, sensitive, and he knew when to listen. Most importantly her parents enjoyed his company, he was related through his previous marriage and they clearly accepted him as a worthy suitor.

She was prepared to leave the answers to the difficult questions to her father, satisfied that Lewis would make her a suitable companion and convinced that such experience and sophistication as he exuded would open the door to a wider world than that which she had previously experienced. 'The aspiration to achieve companionate marriage based on mutual affection, respect and love was pervasive.'[6]

In fact, by then her father had the settlement drawn up ready for signing by the appointed trustees; Uncle Carrington, the Reverend Charles Tayler, Lewis's cousin by marriage, and her step-brother John.[7]

Lewis Agassiz applied for a licence to marry Sarah Eliza Nunn on 14 February 1827.[8] Romantic Lewis chose St Valentine's Day to seal their joint fates. Sarah Eliza celebrated her twenty-first birthday just three days later.

8 The Bride

Monday 19 February 1827 was destined to be Eliza's first day of grown-up life.[1] Monday was the first day the church was available for weddings that week.

> *Monday for Health, Tuesday for Wealth, Wednesday Best Day of all, Thursday for Crosses, Friday for Losses, Saturday, No luck at all.*

"G'd morning Miss, it's a crisp'n again!" The maid set down the tea tray and pulled the heavy drapes aside. Eliza opened her eyes, fully expecting the morning to reveal a sodden landscape drenched by teeming rain.

"Oh it's not raining!" Eliza sat up and squinted in the thin shaft of winter sunlight that streaked across her bed. It was a white frosty day. Her maid looked a little perplexed.

"No, of course it ain't Miss, why'd you be thinkin' of rain?"

"I dreamed of mud! That mud would be the remembrance of my wedding day – and that I would have to wear my walking boots instead of my satin slippers. But look, its bright and clear!"

The maid prevented her from leaping out of bed to peer out the window, by thrusting the tray onto her lap.

"My word, it's a cold'n Miss, so you just stay put a few more min's 'til I've lit yon fire. You'll no' be havin' a streamin' red nose on yer 'oneymoon."

"Mr Agassiz hasn't mentioned a honeymoon. I'm sure he'll say there's no point going on one. The roads will be impassable out of Essex at the moment, as they always are in winter." Eliza held her cup in both hands. "You're right. A running nose would be the final straw!" She sighed. "Winter! Why am I being wed in winter? It's freezing out there."

Eliza poured herself another cup of tea and sipped it gratefully. She had suffered a restless night, bothered by a few last minute qualms. Lying awake in the darkness, all sorts of problems had come to mind, the lack of fresh flowers being one of them. "What flowers shall I have? There are none to be had in the garden except snowdrops. How awful they would be!" Snowdrops made her think of cemeteries. "There's certainly no chance of orange blossom and I don't want artificial flowers either."

When her thoughts moved on to the wedding service, she felt more disquiet.

> *Wilt thou obey him, and serve him; love, honour and keep him; in sickness and in health and, forsaking all others, keep thee only unto him, so long as ye both shall live?*

Eliza listened to the vows at her father's wedding but she was only fourteen then and she had not dwelt on them at her sister's nuptials either. Now facing marriage herself she considered them in a different light. Could she, would she follow them through? Her obligations as a wife were clearly understood.

The childhood governess had required her charges learn the expected wifely virtues by rote.[2] Eliza's memory brought the list clearly to her sleepy mind. Chastity and sobriety were not a problem worth considering – her upbringing allowed for nothing less.

"Industry and frugality sound ominous; I do hope Lewis won't turn out a penny pincher." She was unsure whether she wanted to dwell on the implications of thrift and hard work.

"I know he's cut back on the staff since Elizabeth passed away but hopefully he'll rectify that." Cleanliness and knowledge of domestic affairs she could achieve.

"That leaves good temper and beauty. Lewis wouldn't have proposed if he wasn't satisfied with those."

As the weak sunlight of a wintery morning penetrated the room, it seemed ridiculous to have entertained such doubts. "Well if it were raining, I wouldn't be foolish enough to ruin a pair of slippers for want of sense. I really would wear boots to my wedding." That thought made her smile.

"I wonder what Lewis would think of me walking down the aisle in mud-splotched boots?" She voiced her thoughts out loud as the maid began to brush her hair.

"Miss Eliza, why'd you do that? You've only to step out of the carriage and through yon gate." Not being party to the progress of Eliza's mind, the girl was a little confused by such an idea. "The church path'll be cleared long before you arrive so you needn't to fret over a li'le snow."

One hundred strokes of the hairbrush had marked the beginning and close of every day that Eliza could remember. Today, though it began the same, would end differently to any other she had ever experienced. The dress hanging before her signified that.

There were many tasks to be done in preparation for her new life. Consequently the last few weeks had been an industrious time. The first duty, once the date was set, was her stepmother's responsibility. Marianne handwrote the invitations for the forthcoming nuptials. The expensive sheets of paper bearing her elegant script and Thomas's seal were duly delivered. They were answered politely in kind. It wasn't to be a large wedding. Lewis was quite particular on that.

Eliza usually found a few new gowns a year to be adequate so she was grateful to her Father for suggesting she order another dress for her wedding. She took considerable care over deciding on a design, returning to the last few issues of Ackermann's for inspiration. As she flicked through the pages, Eliza found she was distracted by the romance stories she'd read before Christmas. She allowed herself to dream a little, and then brought herself to task.

She fixed the style in her mind, did a few sketches and the dress was ordered. The lace took some deciding, since the seamstress had such a good variety to select from, and several fittings were required, but it was delivered on time by Manningtree's mantua-maker. It was exquisite. The silk fitted perfectly – an experienced seamstress herself, Eliza could not fault it. She was thrilled to be wearing it.

8 The Bride

Gifts from various relatives began arriving as soon as the invitations were delivered. A parcel of carefully stitched linen-ware arrived by mail from her Aunt Harriot in London. The aunt was unable to attend the wedding, but it was thoughtful of her to send the gift and a little unexpected as Eliza had not seen her since she was a child.[3]

When Eliza invited her friends for tea on her birthday, they expected to view her new possessions. So she laid out the gifts for all to see. The silver tea service took pride of place in the centre of the table, a gift from her parents.

"That punch bowl looks rather elegant Eliza, was there not one similar in the quarterly?"

"Oh I do like the design on the tea cups."

The cousins admired the crystal glasses and a matching decanter from her Uncle Carrington.

In the meantime Eliza stitched herself new petticoats, several new chemises and some additional nightgowns. Though she had been hemming sheets and pillowcases, in preparation for marriage, for many years, Marianne and her father took her to Colchester to purchase supplementary supplies for her trousseau.

The entire family accompanied them on that expedition, her sister and John Ayles included. The little girls had their New Year shillings to spend and Marianne loved the excuse to pursue new fripperies. Thomas was unusually indulgent and generous with his purse that day.

Eliza finished her shopping in possession of a vast supply of new stockings and two new bonnets. She and her sister enjoyed rummaging through ribbons and laces to find the perfect trimmings for their caps and petticoats, for Mary quickly decided it was a good opportunity to replace some of her own dainty adornments as well.

With the arrival of her wedding day, Eliza knew that the time for worrying was over. The preparations were complete, as much as they would ever be. She put down her cup and reached for the latest edition of Ackermann's. She had seen something she particularly liked and thumbed through the pages to find it.

8 The Bride

"Here's the picture. This is the hair style I was considering, can it be done?" She read out the detailed instructions as her maid worked.

14 Wedding Dress, Ackermann's Repository of Arts, January 1827

"The hair is parted in front and has three very large curls on the left side; above are bows of white satin and crepe lisse: sprigs of myrtle and two full-blown roses adorn the right. We will have to leave out the roses, roses in February – only in dreams. I should have bought wax ones in Colchester."

8 The Bride

"We'll find somethin' nice Miss Eliza – I'll send the boy for a stem of somethin', maybe laburnum? Flowers'll be the last thing after you're fully dressed."

Eliza's hair was securely pinned and the three large curls achieved with the aid of a little bandoline to fix them in position. The maid fastened Eliza's corset over her shift and then helped her with the petticoats. Carefully laid across the bed, the gown glowed enticingly, waiting.

"And what'll you wear up'n your neck Miss? Pearls'd look best in me 'umble apinion, but you've none of your own've you?" the girl enquired.

"Oh dear, I hadn't thought." That was something else that had slipped her mind in the preparations. The wedding illustration in front of her displayed a triple string of pearls.

"Father gave Mother's pearls to Mary at her wedding, being the eldest. I will have to ask Marianne to borrow hers I suppose." As if by way of answer there was a light tap at the door and Marianne came in.

"How's the bride feeling today?" she asked. "Mr Agassiz has just been by and delivered a few packages for you my dear. I'm perishing with suspense waiting to see what the surprises are."

Eliza took the boxes and paused. She would have preferred a little privacy at that moment. As she lifted the lid on the smallest one, the three women held their breath. Lying on the dark red velvet was an amber cross, not large, not small, just beautiful, and so perfect.

"Well, it'll do Miss, I 'spec. It's not my place to say anythin'," sniffed the maid, unable to hide her disappointment.

"I love it!" Eliza replied, "It solves our problem completely." What would be in the larger box? She opened it and smiled, her maid would not understand this gift either.

"So romantic! Wild flowers: the first signs of spring."

Yes, Lewis had been out early that morning collecting weeds for his bride to be: beribboned primroses and cheerful crocuses lay in the box, tied together in a nosegay. Fortunately, though they were

82

8 The Bride

not what Eliza had imagined for her wedding day, she was feeling bright enough to realise how apt they were.

"Life without you would be intolerable," the card said, for that was what the primroses signified. That was touching, she hadn't realised Lewis understood the meaning of flowers.

Somehow a bunch of wild flowers garnered from the fields that they had spent autumn wandering through together, dissolved her final worries and cares. Eliza felt confident in her decision to marry a man who could be so thoughtful.

15 Mistley Church

At eleven that morning, Thomas Nunn strode up the aisle of his family church with his radiant daughter on his arm, well pleased to be giving her away to a man he respected and admired. The pair halted at Lewis's side and Eliza turned to her groom. She lifted her bouquet as she met his eyes, noting the matching posy on his lapel, and smiled shyly. "Thank you, it was so thoughtful of you, and such a nice surprise," she mouthed.

"I, Sarah Eliza Nunn take thee Lewis Agassiz to my wedded husband to have and to hold from this day forward, for better, for worse, for richer, for poorer, in sickness and in health, to love and to cherish, and to obey, till death us do part, according to God's holy ordinance; and thereto I give thee my troth."

It was said, and Lewis beamed through his own vows in response. Regardless of her nerves, he was relaxed and happy: happier than Eliza had seen him in over a year. The familiar bells of the church began ringing as organ music accompanied the couple down the aisle. Rice splattered down over their heads at the doorway.

A quick dash to the carriage followed and the party set out for the wedding breakfast at Thomas's expense. A banquet of champagne and wedding cake was Eliza's memory of the meal. With the toasts over and Lewis's pledges made to her father, Eliza found herself seated in Lewis's barouche driving up the hill towards her new abode, Stour Lodge.

The first days the pair had been completely alone together were spent there at Stour Lodge. Lewis had wondered how she would be. They were the first days that Eliza had ever been separated from her family. Eliza wondered how he would adapt to another woman in his life too but her anxiety was set aside. Sarah Eliza Agassiz surprised them both with how relaxed and comfortable she was, in fact she was happy – wildly, wonderfully happy.

Lewis did manage to whisk Eliza away to the coast for a few days in spring, just a little vacation, since he did not want Elizabeth to feel lonesome or in the slightest way supplanted in his affections. He promised Eliza that they would take a journey to the continent later in the year when the weather improved.

By the time they returned home, Eliza held a few suspicions, and then she was certain.

"Lewis I am, that is, I have a hope…" What was the best way to tell him? "I am entertaining the hope of becoming a mother in the near future!"

9 The Newly Weds

Quickly deciding that Stour Lodge was a good size to manage, Eliza approached her new household responsibilities with enthusiasm and dedication. She looked upon her new home as a dolls' house, it was pretty enough to be such. Eliza knew that Lewis and Elizabeth had worked hard at making it comfortable. She was proud to show it off to her friends and her sisters.

There were many callers in those first months of marriage, especially as the days began to warm. Eliza's friends and cousins all visited Stour Lodge in response to the formal cards sent out after the wedding. It was a way of acknowledging her new station in life.

Eliza, wearing her wedding dress, as was the custom for such visits, took the opportunity to air her new silver tea service. She entertained, with grace and decorum, in the drawing room so that her visitors could enjoy the splendid view across the Stour Estuary. After each party, Eliza insisted on carefully washing and drying her china herself, seated at the table in the morning room as her stepmother and grandmother had done.

Spring soon gave way to summer but Eliza still preferred to entertain inside. She was reluctant to take her precious china outdoors. Besides, Lewis's trees were not yet large enough to offer good shade on the lawn.

"It's such a fine afternoon. Who will join me for a turn in the garden?"

Lewis would take the visitors outside after tea if the weather permitted such activity, for a game of what he termed 'pall mall' or some archery on the lawn. He was keen that they admired the precincts of his house.[1]

9 The Newly Weds

Eliza had to concede that the garden was special. It added to the prettiness of the outlook over the fields and meadows that rolled down towards the estuary. It had been cultivated from a farm field in 1823 when the house was completed. Four summers later, it was flourishing. Everyone noticed Lewis's animation whenever he began to discuss his borders.

Before her marriage, Eliza listened politely to endless descriptions of the bushes and bulbs that he purchased for the old fashioned parterre. At the time, the adolescent had found such detailed accounts monotonous. However, she was grateful that she had paid attention then. Nowadays she had an appreciation of how important it was to him.

"Lewis, I do love the house but I'd like to make it something of my own. I was wondering about curtains."

"I'd rather not alter anything just yet Eliza, the curtains are all new. Elizabeth never stinted on quality."

"I understand Lewis, but I would really like something yellow for the morning room. My allowance will cover the cost. They would make a bright start to the day." With her husband's reluctant consent, Eliza quickly set about ordering the drapes before he changed his mind.[2]

The small domestic staff already established in the household, were obliging enough and ready to indulge her, pleased as they were to have a new mistress. They held her husband in great respect. Eliza was satisfied that they obeyed her, despite her keenly felt youth and inexperience. Her lady's maid accompanied her from Thomas's house – it was a comfort to have someone who understood her preferences and needs. There was a daily woman who carried the burden of cleaning and the cook lived in the cottage next door.

Laundry day, once a fortnight, was Eliza's biggest hurdle. That required her full attention. With such a small household, Lewis plainly desired to avoid the expense of a laundry maid.

Though being careful with his expenditure, Lewis kept two vehicles in the chaise house. One was a small gig, mainly for his own use. Eliza hoped he would allow her to learn to drive this. He also kept a 'sociable'.[3] This was an open barouche with seating for four. It had a folding hood and was drawn by a matching pair.

Lewis was always ready for a drive, so he was very happy to accompany her on calls. Indeed, in those early months of marriage it would have been considered impolite if he had not.

As well as the new house to organise and the proper post-wedding visitations to complete, Eliza had other things on her mind. Her corsets soon needed loosening as the quickening in her belly confirmed her expectation.

"Does anyone know of a good nursemaid?" Eliza enquired of her female friends one afternoon. That called everyone's attention and congratulations abounded.

"You'll be looking for a monthly nurse first and a wet nurse perhaps?" Her stepmother was quick to show her interest.

"No a wet nurse won't be necessary," Eliza was decisive on that point. "Just a nursemaid is all we want." Lewis had been involved in that decision.[4]

Plenty of well-meaning advice and many old wives tales were offered. Eliza found herself permitted to matronly conversations of childbirth experiences. Quite a few of the stories sounded rather frightening. 'Doubtless, all pregnant women knew of someone who had died in childbed and no one could guarantee that they would not be the next.'[5]

Eliza was as young and healthy as she could possibly be. The experienced village physician promised to attend the delivery. He advised her to eat well, to avoid horse riding and to make sure she enjoyed some daily fresh air.

Eliza and Lewis were well aware of the dangers she faced. They had both been 'brought up by the spoon,' deprived of their natural mother's care as infants. 'No one could predict how easily she would bear pregnancy, how safely she would deliver, how robust would be her infant, or how long and healthy the life of her child.'[6]

The newlyweds were optimistic. They agreed to do their best to avoid dwelling on the hazards that childbirth presented. Fortitude and resignation were required.

9 The Newly Weds

It was not long before Eliza's thoughts were entirely taken up by the practical needs heralded by the imminent arrival of their child. There was much to prepare. The nursery, established when the house was built, was well thought out and nicely furnished. It already contained Elizabeth Mary Ann's crib bed and there were a few baby things left over from her infancy.

Eliza set herself to preparing a layette, the countless vests and gowns that would be needed later in the year. Every woman she knew seemed to have guidance to offer – the requirements were dauntingly endless. She used her smallest, daintiest stitches for the tiny caps, nightgowns, day gowns, and chemises. They were all cut from soft cotton lawn, the seams being kept to a minimum, as small and smooth as she could make them so they would not rub the skin of her infant. Lewis showed an indulgent interest in the items she was collecting in the nursery.

"They don't look very warm for a winter baby," he ran the fabric between his fingers doubtfully.

"These warm flannels go over the shirts." She showed him the long woollen barracoats that would provide an insulating layer between the fine soft chemises, embroidered cotton petticoats and even more elaborate gowns.

"Next I need to hem the napkins. There will be dozens of them. I bought a bolt of diaper weave cotton last week, perhaps you wondered what that bundle was that we brought back from Colchester. I still have to make up the pilchers. They need to be waterproof. And then there are the binders to sew."[7]

"What, in heaven's name, is a binder? It sounds a little barbaric."

"Do you not remember Elizabeth wearing one?"

"I never saw her undressed, the nurse took care of her clothes," replied Lewis. Lewis regretted that he had not been more involved in his daughter's nursery days. She was growing up fast.

"They're really very important," Eliza explained seriously. In her father's home, she had helped to bathe and dress Marianne's baby girls. She gave Lewis the explanation told to her by her little stepsisters' old nurse.

9 The Newly Weds

"The cloth wraps around the infant's body to support the weak bones and keep the bowels warm. It helps the umbilical cord to heal into a nice smooth, inverted dent. That's quite imperative. I've made an addition to it though. See, I have sewn ties on the ends of each of them so I won't have to use pins so close to baby's body. Don't you think that is a good idea?"

The 'long clothes' for Eliza's new-born baby had skirts of forty inches in length which meant plenty of covering for tiny bare legs and feet. 'Short clothes' were set aside until the infant started crawling. These gowns were considerably less cumbersome, limited to ankle length and combined with socks and stockings for warmth. A cape and bonnet completed the outfit for any outdoor expedition.

Meanwhile, Lewis continued compiling his plans for a trip to the continent. He initially hoped the journey would take place in the first year of their marriage and accordingly sold his yacht that September. However with a child on the way his plans had been laid aside for a time.

Time flew past very quickly for Eliza. As her body grew, she became more content. By Advent, she was confined to home completely – she was officially 'in retirement' with all outings suspended.

On 24 December, 1827, Eliza was safely delivered of a son. Lewis Nunn Agassiz was welcomed by his father with great delight and pride.

Shortly after Lewis Nunn's birth, another reason presented itself for the delay of their continental journey. Robert Nunn was gravely ill. Lewis was close to his erstwhile father-in-law and did not want to abandon the old man.

There was a mercenary motive for remaining at Robert's side; a nagging suspicion that Elizabeth's cousins might try to have his will revised, if he, Lewis, was absent. Consequently, Lewis visited the old man's bedside, as often as he could, over the next few months.

Robert died in June 1828. Most of his wealth was bequeathed to Elizabeth Mary Ann.[8] Eliza's stepdaughter was now the heiress to a substantial fortune.

9 The Newly Weds

By the time of her Great Uncle's passing, Eliza realised that their small family would again be increasing in size. The wedding trip was delayed once more. For the second year running there was no mistletoe to be seen at Stour Lodge at Christmastime. There was plenty of rejoicing, nevertheless. Lewis and Eliza were celebrating the birth of their second son – on his brother's birthday. Arthur James John was named for his Great Uncle Arthur and Grandfather, James John Charles Agassiz.[9]

At nine years of age, young Elizabeth was cautiously happy with the appearance of two tiny brothers. As Lewis Nunn and Arthur gained mobility she discovered several drawbacks to having siblings. A few swift rescues of her dolls saw her removed from the nursery to a separate schoolroom for daytime hours. Lewis employed a governess to oversee her education. Eliza's time was too taken up with the little ones, to continue with that. The nursemaid was an essential, well-established member of the household also. Though Eliza was careful to mind her children herself, she was grateful for the help.[10]

Eliza's duties and cares increased quickly in the early years of marriage. She was obliged to spend whatever spare moments she had stitching new clothes for her rapidly growing boys. There was no time to spend in the kitchen helping Cook anymore. With two babies in the house, washday became a more frequent occurrence, one which Eliza could no longer manage alone. Lewis finally agreed to employ a laundry maid from the village.

10 The Travellers

The entire household was in upheaval. With their departure date looming, Eliza was preparing for the family's forthcoming expedition. Completing the arrangements was becoming an endless, daunting task. She continued working through her packing list. It seemed to be lengthening as she worked.

"I wonder if Mr Agassiz realises just how much luggage is required by four women, a child and two infants," she mused as she worked down the page. Addressing her maid, she continued her thoughts aloud.

"We don't want to make the Master cross about too much luggage so we shall have to be quite careful about what we pack."

Sarah Eliza Agassiz tried not to give in to the increasing agitation she was feeling. There were many unknowns and with two little children she needed to be prepared for every eventuality. The nursemaid seemed to have worked herself into quite a state too. There were incessant questions and complaints.

"What'll I do 'bout the clouts, Ma'am?"

"We shall make sure we take plenty, dozens and dozens of course," she replied as evenly as she could manage.

The babies' napkins were the least of her concerns and she certainly was not going to let such a trivial matter disrupt the exciting expedition.

"But two babes and sixteen days of travel, how many'll we need for that?" The whimpering voice continued. "Will we be able to wash them?"

Eliza had already given some thought to that.

"If we take several lidded pails in the coach, and change the water every night, I'm sure it will be quite simple to rinse them out whenever we have opportunity. The motion of the carriage will help clean them, besides." She thought she had found a solution.

"That's a good idea Ma'am," the nursemaid nodded approval.

Then, just in case the girl had the wrong idea she continued.

"Mind now, you mustn't think that you can stint on changing the boys. You know they'll suffer rashes if we leave them too long. I just hope we'll have facilities to give them a decent wash every day." Before the maid could interrupt, she changed the subject.

"How are you getting on with Elizabeth's trunk?" The maid glanced up to catch Eliza's questioning look.

"Ma'am? I haven't started that yet."

"A couple of travelling dresses and one morning gown should be sufficient for her. She's growing so fast there is no point taking too much. But do make sure you put in ample supplies of drawers and petticoats. They won't take very much space. We'll leave the horsehair underskirts behind; they'll be too uncomfortable to travel in and too bulky to pack. I think her red cape and bonnet would be best for the carriage."

There was much more to keep Eliza busy besides packing. Etiquette required that she visit her relatives to take farewell of them all. It came as quite a relief when she could finally relax and chat with her sister. Being of a naturally sunny, light-hearted disposition, Mary had the knack of distracting her from her concerns. She was simply uninterested in the details.

"Just think, in a fortnight's time you'll be shopping in Paris, I'm so envious."

"Yes I'm hoping to spruce up my wardrobe. My newest dresses were made up before our wedding and I'm not the same shape that I was then." Eliza did like to keep up with the mode.

"But perhaps it's being overly optimistic to expect to go shopping," she replied a little wistfully. "Mr Agassiz probably won't have included it in his schedule and it definitely won't fit in with his budget. He has everything worked out so carefully."

Though he had a generous allowance from Elizabeth's inheritance and a steady, comfortable income, Lewis was obliged to be careful with their finances. Eliza had the returns from her marriage settlement to spend on clothing. Somehow, that was expected to cover the cost of her gowns, her children's garments and the expense of keeping her personal maid. Careful economy was not a new concept for Eliza as her father had been a frugal man, generous when required, but reluctant to pay for unnecessary expenditure.

Lewis's head was full of plans and figures. Consequently, the travel arrangements dominated their mealtime conversations. He prepared the itinerary with the help of an agent, a *voiturier*, who was engaged on the recommendation of his uncle.

Lewis's uncle initially suggested the idea of visiting Switzerland. Uncle Arthur, brother to Lewis's father, had visited his son who lived in a château near Geneva.[1] He described the beautiful scenery and the cheap living. Lewis had been impressed and read his uncle's correspondence aloud to his wife.

"Tell me why we are headed to Lausanne in particular Lewis," Eliza probed her husband for more information, sometimes she noticed he needed a little prompting to explain himself.

"Why are we not going to Lucerne or Geneva?" She had read Percy Shelley's account of a tour through Switzerland; the book was in Lewis's library. "The Shelley's had little to say of Lausanne."[2]

"My family roots are there. Grandfather told me so much of the Vaud where he was born.[3] I want to get a real sense of the place, not just pay a fleeting visit. It is supposed to be quite breath-taking, with beautiful views. There are vast ranges of towering mountains above the town. Their reflections can be seen in the clear blue lake below. 'Le Paradis de la Suisse' is how my uncle described it." The scenery was not the only reason for the visit to Lausanne.

"More importantly, I have heard that Lausanne offers quite the best schooling that is available for young ladies. There are several respectable establishments to choose from and they charge as little as a quarter of London prices."[4]

10 The Travellers

While the prospect of some snipe shooting with Cousin Arthur interested Lewis, what he was more concerned about was Elizabeth Mary Ann's education. Lewis was very aware of his responsibilities in bringing his little heiress up in a manner suited to her situation. Onto his pet subject now, he continued.

"A good governess is all very well as a companion for my little girl," he declared, "but I want Elizabeth to be clever at much more than the usual ladylike activities. I think the mastery of several languages is essential."

He was anxious to have her French improve. "I'm disappointed with the governess's French accent, it is most unnaturally affected. I believe Elizabeth's pronunciation will do better with native instruction. Reliable governesses are difficult to find, so I would not change her for that. It is the good woman's only failing." Since Lewis was quite prone to finding fault, this was quite a recommendation for his conscientious employee.

The initial plan was that they would take the northern route to the continent, sailing from Harwich to spend some time in the pretty Flanders city of Bruges.[5] However, Lewis was warned of civil unrest in Belgium.

The alteration of his plans, to a departure from Dover, meant a quicker passage, over calmer waters, than crossing the North Sea would be. Eliza was relieved, neither she nor any of her servants had ever travelled by boat before so they had yet to prove their sea legs. It was logical they would take a few days in London on the way to Dover.

"Do you think we might travel across to Lewisham, to visit my mother's old home? I know it's been sold but I remember it to be quite spectacular. You would be impressed. And I would love to meet my Aunt Harriot to thank her for the wedding gift in person. I think they still live in Southwark. Papa will know."[6]

Lewis was doubtful about that but promised to ask Thomas if he retained contact with any members of the Nicholson family. Lewis planned a few days of educational sightseeing in London. He particularly wanted to show Elizabeth the interior of St Paul's

10 The Travellers

Cathedral and he was reluctant to waste time visiting relatives if that could be avoided.

The party of eight travellers including Lewis, his wife, his daughter, two infants, a governess and two female servants, departed from Dover aboard a steamer at eleven on 6 April 1829.[7] The morning was clear and bright. Close to shore, while the sea was smooth, the passengers all enjoyed the views of the white cliffs as they departed England. But as the vessel progressed further into the channel, the wind began to rise and soon the steamer was rolling heavily. The female members of the party hurried into the shelter of the cabin.

16 The Quay at Dover, 1829

Eliza returned to the deck, child on her hip, looking for Lewis. She spotted him with his eyes closed, facing into the wind. He was probably reliving the exhilarating feeling of sharp salty gusts that he remembered from his midshipman days she thought. Lewis looked so relaxed that Eliza hesitated to disturb him, however the needs of the women below were pressing. His support was necessary.

Eliza tugged his arm and broke into his reverie.

"Lewis, I know it is a great deal to ask, but could you take care of little Lew please? The governess and both the maids are already prone with illness."

That made Lewis groan, he had little patience with the sufferers of seasickness.

"I have my hands full taking care of them as well as the baby. You know I wouldn't ask for help unless it was imperative."

Lewis was not particularly happy at being disturbed and he was less happy at having the squirming toddler thrust into his arms, but he was always alarmed when his eldest daughter might be at risk.

"Elizabeth? Is she alright?"

"Yes, yes, she is in good spirits. She's minding the baby as we speak. She wanted to come up to you but I could hardly allow her up on deck unaccompanied, and it's too breezy for Arthur so I insisted she stay below and take care of him. Now I really must get back down. Here you are." She was firm with her husband, "Little Lew will enjoy seeing the boats with his father."

Little Lew had new boots since he had just learned to walk. At first, that is what Little Lew intended to do. He squirmed and twisted in his father's arms with the determination of a toddler, and made it clear that he did not want to be held.

However, Lewis Nunn Agassiz was soon distracted by the sights to be seen. While his father pointed out boats and discussed their tonnage and rigging, the child waved at the gulls diving amongst the puffs of black steamy smoke that belched out from the boat's funnel. The two and a half hour crossing passed remarkably quickly for the father and son.

It was fortunate for the ladies below that the trip was accomplished with such speed. Arriving in France meant equilibrium was restored for the sea sickness sufferers.

In Calais, Eliza prompted Lewis to begin writing a travel journal.

"But Eliza, what shall I write?" He shrugged his shoulders. "There is nothing here that strikes me as worthy of recording, and besides the days will be busy enough."

"Lewis, write for those who might follow in your footsteps. Write of the 'dense and motley crowds' that we negotiated this afternoon and how we came to present our passports at the Hotel de Ville – you know it was difficult to find the information you needed for our travels yourself."

The family set off towards Paris the next morning. There, Lewis spent three days sight-seeing and visiting old acquaintances. Eliza longed to join him but her responsibility was to care for her little ones. She had to stay behind to see that the washing was brought up to date and make sure of preparations for the further trip ahead. They managed a few outings as a family, including a walk along the Seine and a trip to the zoo.

She took the opportunity to write to her sister.

> *You will see by the postmark that we have arrived in Paris. I am relieved to have a few days of respite. I had no idea how long the journey we have undertaken was going to be. Lewis told me today that it is more than six hundred miles from Mistley to Lausanne. Do not misunderstand me sister. Long and tiring the days in the coach might be, but I enjoy the travelling. I have time to think and play games with little Lew. The children are well. I thought the strangeness of the food might bother them, but they seem unaffected by it.*
>
> *Despite Lewis's high expectations and sound preparation, it has not been a trouble-free undertaking. Numerous inconveniences present every day. The chief complaint, next to the unimaginably rough roads, is of the filthy conveniences we endure at the inns along the way. I cannot bear to describe them to you.*
>
> *Our grievances are only trifles but I can see the strain of tending a coach full of females is telling on Lewis. Poor man, he tries hard to be patient with all of us and he always puts the needs of his delicate infants first. He has lost his temper several times with the coachman. He 'gave our gentleman a good rowing.'*[4] *(Lewis appears to be suspicious of the French dear Sister. He is always expecting exploitation.)*

In his defence, I must say that many of the little headaches we face would never have bothered him if he were travelling on his own or with other men.

You will be disappointed to hear that I have been unable to do any shopping, though dear Lewis promises me that he will make amends on the return trip, whenever that will be.

Eliza had to choose her words carefully if there was a problem. Completely reliant on Lewis's provisioning, she had to make sure her children had their needs met without causing friction. She recognised that he took pride in having everything in hand and consequently avoided bothering him if she could.

They were all tired, unused to travelling as they were. Eliza, though cheerful and enjoying the novelty of ever-changing scenery, nevertheless found the journey a challenge. As well as the children to keep content and quiet she kept a close eye on her servants to make sure they completed their allotted tasks every evening. Eliza could not risk upsetting them. Neither could she allow a hint of how weary she was herself. The women were further from home than they had ever been before. Travelling was difficult for them.

The babes seemed unaffected by the long days of travel. Just a few months old, baby Arthur slept contentedly for a large part of each day, lulled to sleep by the swaying of the carriage. By the time little Lew could be persuaded to take a nap in his wicker basket, the maids were happy to relax into slumber too. That gave Eliza pleasant time to think and drift off should she choose to.

"He's such an angel when he's asleep; so gorgeous with his thumb sticking out of his mouth and his beloved doll tucked in beside him," Eliza voiced her pride to no one in particular as she admired her eldest son peacefully asleep in his blankets.

Elizabeth was perfectly happy. Eliza did not have to worry about her. When the weather allowed, she joined her father outside in the fresh air. He enjoyed her company. She was quite fascinated by the villages they passed through, the rolling countryside and even the other carriages on the roads. Really, everything about the expedition appealed to the girl.

10 The Travellers

Lewis talked to her about the vineyards. She in turn pointed out the pretty orchards of peach trees in bloom.

"Papa, do stop the coach. There's Punchinello playing the fool," she cried one day as they passed through a village.[9]

With a new destination attained by the end of each day, Lewis made the most of any remaining daylight to explore on foot. He visited the village markets with Eliza's list of supplies and frequently returned with a funny little story with which to entertain her.

"I haggled some time with an old woman about the price of her eggs; she cheated and I told her so; the detection only produced a hearty laugh in which she was joined by her neighbours," was the substance of one evening's report to his wife.[10]

The travelling became more strenuous as they approached the border between France and Switzerland. The final haul over the Jura was a monumental task which required the ladies alight from the coach and ascend on foot. Then at last, they had their destination in sight and they were rewarded with the views: 'a perpetual change of the most magnificent scenery'.[11]

New sights, new sounds, and new smells awaited them in Lausanne. Their lodgings were near the centre of the town. They were well settled by the time summer arrived and Eliza was soon confidently venturing forth for supplies in the French speaking city.

The ovens of the nearby bakery filled the street with the delicious aroma of fresh warm bread and the rich scent of roasted chicory coffee tempted them into quaint little coffee shops. Wednesday and Saturday were market days. There was an irresistible supply of fresh fish, fruit and vegetables in summer. To have such an assortment of shops so close to their home was a luxury to Eliza.[12]

"Never have I seen so much fruit Lewis, the variety is quite astounding. Today there were apricots, raspberries, gooseberries and red currants for sale. I bought you some grapes, and some pastries too."[13]

"The shops of this city are good," wrote Lewis in his journal that evening, "particularly those of the pastry-cooks of which there are a great number."[14]

10 The Travellers

The views from the city perched on the hill above Lac Leman were as special as Lewis had promised: quite unlike any Eliza had ever seen before and well worth the effort to see them. Of course to attain those views, the steep streets had to be negotiated first. They were especially arduous for an English woman impeded by the tangle of long skirts that Eliza was obliged to wear. She could understand why the Swiss women wore their hems so much shorter.

Lewis noted the 'shortness of petticoat' in his journal too. He also recorded the absence of footpaths.

While Eliza had the children to occupy her, Lewis was free. Keen to make the most of the short summer, he set out on a tour on foot as soon as he was sure the family were settled. Then after a brief summer, winter closed in.

Busy as usual with her household responsibilities, Eliza sent Lewis to the library to research the history of Switzerland. They found a good school for Elizabeth to attend, Lewis very satisfied with the price he paid for it.

The procession of St Nicholas on 6 December began the Swiss-style Christmas celebrations. To decorate the houses there were paper snowflakes and a profusion of white candles. Star-shaped biscuits made from ground almonds, cinnamon and honey were provided as edible treats for well-behaved children. There were steaming cups of hot chocolate and spiced doughnuts for everyone.

On Christmas Eve a procession of children walked through the town. This performance delighted the household. They were led by a child dressed as an angel in white. Crowned for the privilege, he rang a silver bell to herald the arrival of *le petit Jésus*. Eliza held Lew high so that he could see.

"Look Lew, look at the angel! If you're a good boy *le petit Jésus* might bring you presents." Little Lew was not particularly interested in the angel but he squirmed in his mother's arms to get down and join the older children.

The New Year brought snow, plenty of it. Sleds were not used very often in Essex but here they were relied upon for winter outings. The long dark evenings were a time for social gatherings and entertainments. They were invited to a plethora of balls and parties.[15] The Swiss welcomed the English visitors.

Compared to the quiet country events Eliza was used to, the societal evenings of Lausanne were splendid and impressive. The abundance of oil lamps in the streets was another remarkable difference from Essex village life. That made attending functions much easier on dark winter nights.

Eliza's first daughter was born the following summer.[16]

Two months later, the family departed Lausanne after a visit of twenty months duration.[17]

They purchased their own carriage for the journey, preferring to be in control of their timetable and stops. With three little ones to care for now, their return needed to be taken at a leisurely pace, though the travellers had to be mindful of the rapidly encroaching winter. The children's nurse accompanied the family on the journey, along with a Swiss groom, but Eliza and Lewis sent the bulk of their possessions homewards by diligence with their other servants.

Crossing France was not as scenic as the spring trip had been. Eliza read Lewis's journal notes as he wrote one evening and commented on his writing.

"Lewis, you could word it better. Let me have a turn." She wrote a few words and showed him.

> *The delicate green of the vineyards is now completely faded; the lovely peach blossom no longer exists; the grass is withered from the heat of the by-gone summer; and the trees are becoming leafless.*[18]

11 The Travellers Return

Boulogne marked the end of the adventure. The family stopped there for their last night in France.

Eliza had barely seen her husband since the departure from Paris. She was looking forward to a quiet conversation with him that evening. Before that could happen, the children needed to be settled. While Eliza took care of them, Lewis saw to stabling the horses. Once his chores were done, he promised he would join her to enjoy the comfort of the fire.

When he came in, Eliza refrained from suggesting that her husband might wash first. Instead she wordlessly passed him his claret. She hovered, wanting to talk but waiting for his shoulders to relax.

"As good as this burgundy is I think I've developed a taste for the white wines of Lausanne." When Lewis acknowledged her presence, Eliza was relieved. She had noted that after a long day's drive he tended to be a little grumpy, too tired to talk. "Yes, they're fresher, cleaner on the palate. I'm glad we've sent some home."

"Home." Eliza smiled at the reference to their destination. "That's a good word to say isn't it? It will be pleasant to return. I'm so looking forward to seeing Grandfather, and meeting Mary's children. How are you feeling about it? You seemed a little reluctant to depart Paris."

"I've mixed feelings about returning to Mistley Eliza, I have to admit," Lewis nodded.

"I reflected on the year today, while everyone else was asleep. Although I've missed the family, it's been a good experience."

11 The Travellers Return

"Lausanne was a good choice of destination. It was better than I ever expected."

"The anonymity of being a stranger for a while was refreshing."

"We were accepted as ourselves, unimpeded by the past or our connections were we not? And the society was gay and lively compared to the quiet isolation of the Stour Valley." Notwithstanding that, Eliza was looking forward to the peace and tranquillity of home, for a time.

"For me, the best thing about Lausanne was the opportunity to explore – the feeling of adventure was invigorating. It was unbelievably exhilarating to achieve the summits of mountains and be rewarded with such spectacular views."

"There may not be mountains but there are adventures to be had at home Lewis. You'll soon be sailing again. Don't you look forward to that? You must have missed your boats while we were in Switzerland." Eliza knew he missed the water, she had seen the look on his face while he watched the yachts on the lake.

"You might join the hunt as well. I know you've avoided getting out with Father but they would welcome you," she continued.

"I might do that," Lewis replied. Despite the words Eliza thought he sounded indifferent to the idea. He continued, changing the subject. "And you must be looking forward to seeing our garden?"

During the first years of marriage Eliza had found a new diversion in supervising the gardening. At first she was too timid to make changes to Lewis's pride and joy but with his ready encouragement she had all but taken over the responsibility for it.

"All those seeds and cuttings you have tucked away. Do you think they will take?"

"I hope so. I'm considering an alpine rockery at the end of the eastern lawn." He flinched a little at that, wondering if he could bear the alterations that Eliza was contemplating. Since gardening was a joint pleasure he hoped he would be allowed some input into her plans.

"It's a good opportunity to take stock of the flower beds and see if the overall design still suits," Lewis responded cautiously.

11 The Travellers Return

"The orchard will certainly need some work by now. I'm glad we left instructions with the gardener that he was not to prune anything in our absence. It will be interesting to check the growth."

"Yes, I really am looking forward to the first glance of home Lewis. It will be good."

"I'm pleased I've had my own carriage on this trip. It made remarkable economic sense and I'm sure it has been easier upon you and the little ones." Lewis changed the subject. Making decisions about the garden could wait.

"Much better to be driven at our own pace, thank you Lewis, it can't be an easy undertaking for you. It looks like we will complete the journey before the snow too. That's a relief."

There was something else that Eliza wanted to address. "What do you think of a Christmas Eve party Lewis? I want to celebrate our home-coming, Christmas with the family, and the boys' birthdays, all at the same time."

"A party is a good idea, though I'd rather you didn't exhaust yourself with the organising so soon after our arrival. Besides, Marianne may have already made plans. Better ask her first my dear."

The next morning, they departed Calais with their chaise and team stowed safely in the steamer's hold. With the crossing completed, it took several days to complete the journey back to Essex. By then the weather was swiftly deteriorating. The last few days of travel were conducted in monotonously damp, cold conditions.

When Lewis allowed his drenched horses to slow to a walking pace, the change in rhythm was sufficient to stir Eliza from her semi-doze. She had been contemplating the situation of her poor husband outside. Eliza could picture his shoulders hunched low into his greatcoat against the dreary drizzle. She shifted the weight of the slumbering child to her other arm and reached up to wipe the window pane. To her surprise, they were passing through familiar territory, closer to home than she had dared hope. Lewis must have decided to press on instead of taking a break in Colchester.

11 The Travellers Return

"Wake up! Wake up! We're almost home!"

Within a few more minutes, she pointed out Mistley's church to her children. Its towers were just peeking through the grey mist that was rolling off the mud of the estuary beyond. Wide-awake now the little boys obediently peered out. Their pudgy hands waved frantically as the vehicle negotiated the village, surprising any inhabitant who happened to have braved the miserable weather. The final leg of the journey was uphill. Ten minutes later the team steered left off the road into the gentle curve of the drive.

The carriage door opened before any of the family had realised they had drawn to a halt. Marianne and Thomas were awaiting their arrival.

"Welcome home my little ones!"

Marianne certainly did have plans and she was quick to announce them upon the family's arrival. Mary and John were already settled with her and Thomas for the duration of the festive season. Once Eliza's family had unpacked, they were to join the Nunn's on Christmas Eve.

At Eliza's prompting, Lewis rewarded the travel-weary maids for their faithful attendance with an extra half-crown and allowed them the rare treat of a few days to visit their families in the village over Christmas. They were undeniably pleased to return home – to be enfolded into the familiar comfort of village life. The foreign language, strange customs, as well as the exhausting travel involved, had tested the nerve of these country girls. Very few of the villagers had travelled to distant and exotic lands as they had done and everyone was anxious to hear their stories.

There was a special cake to celebrate Eliza's boys' joint birthday on the 24th. They marked the occasion surrounded by family, the household a cacophony of crying babies and demanding toddlers.

Mary had two children; her eldest daughter was a few months younger than Lewis Nunn, and her son just over a year old.[1] Thomas and Marianne's daughters, aged six and eight, had grown remarkably. Henrietta and Matilda, with a full grasp of language, seemed to have incessant squabbles. Their father ignored them, he was used to daughters and such behaviour, but Marianne seemed to be constantly intervening.

"Come downstairs children, come and meet your cousins." Mary collected her pair from the nursery.

"Don't be shy Mary Anne, say hello." Faced with strangers, the little girl found her mother's skirts a good place to hide.

Eliza's boys, well used to the unfamiliar, were rather more confident. The little fellows solemnly held out their hands and introduced themselves as they had seen their father do. Having been promised playmates, Lewis and Arthur were keen to make their cousins' acquaintance. At the ages of three and two it was no bother to them that one was a girl and the other little more than a baby.

Eliza and Mary admired each other's progeny.

"Hello, little John, I'm very pleased to meet you. My, don't you look like your father now." Mary's pride in her son was evident. Eliza's approbation was welcome.

Elizabeth Mary Ann was eleven years old and quite the young lady. Being fresh from her exclusive education at a Swiss Establishment, and conscious of her new grown up corset, she was too dignified to join little girl games. On this special occasion she was allowed to remain with the women after the other children were whisked out of sight.

Eliza traced the familiar pattern that decorated the china of her stepmother's tea set. It was another reminder of how good it was to be home. The ladies settled themselves comfortably in the drawing room. There was much catching up to do: stories of Eliza's travels and Mary's tales of gossip were interspersed with their mothering experiences.

"They're so different aren't they? Little boys and girls I mean. Don't you find that?"

"Never mind the children Eliza. Let me admire your new silk; fancy owning a Parisian gown. How fine you look in that. I am so envious."

"I have something for you two ladies. Elizabeth, will you bring them over please?"

11 The Travellers Return

Elizabeth had been lingering nearby with Eliza's reticule, waiting for that moment. She presented Marianne and Mary with a small parcel each. Paper wrappings rapidly discarded, the gifts were held up and admired. The silk and tortoiseshell fans purchased in Paris were exquisite. Elizabeth and Eliza had taken great care in choosing the hand painted designs.

17 The French Fans, 1835, Courier des Salons

11 The Travellers Return

While the women caught up on seemingly inconsequential trivialities, Thomas herded the men off to his library as soon as he could manage - the gentlemen had serious business to discuss.

"I'm keen to hear your thoughts on the state of the nation," Lewis began.

His friends had plenty to say on the subject. The reigns of the Hanoverian Georges had finally ended during their absence with the death of King George IV. That had brought about the dissolving of parliament earlier in the year. William was soon to be crowned and Earl Charles Grey had become Prime Minister, the head of a Whig Government. Grey had pledged to carry out parliamentary reforms – a somewhat disconcerting idea to the elite of the nation. The gentlemen landholders of the Stour Estuary were anticipating change.

Lewis had much to report of his travels. He also had some ideas for a business venture that he wanted to put to his relatives. He had brought back a stock of wine from Switzerland for the purpose. He knew John was interested in wine.

The family settled back into their country ways and Eliza's life reverted into its old patterns. She noticed that little had altered in twenty months. The faces she encountered were all familiar: friends, relatives, tradesmen and merchants remained unchanged. No new buildings had been erected and none removed. The curtains in the village windows were the same as before their departure and even the ruts in the road had not altered in the interim.

Managing the house and children absorbed the days. Then there was the garden to see to. That took patience to set to rights. At first, in the middle of winter, the beds looked forlorn and sleepy but with the warmer weather, and many hours of dedicated work from a locally employed gardener, the garden recovered. By spring it was glowing again, so was Eliza. She was expecting another child.

How Lewis adjusted to the confinements of their rural life was of concern to his young wife. Being occupied with the household and her children herself, Eliza was relieved when her brother-in-law found a yacht for sale, which met with Lewis's approval.

11 The Travellers Return

John Ayles, having inherited portions of his family's ship-building business was generally held to be the expert in nautical matters. Lewis purchased the *Betsey* at the end of 1831 just a few weeks before the birth of their third son.[2]

Rodolph's birth in January 1832 prevented Eliza's attending her brother's wedding. Young Tom's new wife, Maria Nunn, was a near neighbour and second cousin to Eliza, the daughter of her Great Uncle William. Maria had been brought up at Nether Hall just across the fields from Stour Lodge so she was a frequent caller at their house in the early days of Eliza's marriage.[3] Eliza had to be content with depending on Lewis to furnish the details of the occasion.

Both her brother and sister married close relatives. Though it was normal for the elite of that tiny community to marry amongst their cousins, Eliza could not help be reminded how fortunate she was to have been allowed to wed an outsider. Eliza was only too aware of how restrictive life in the country was. She was privileged to have escaped for a short time to have enjoyed her continental adventure.

There were sometimes advantages to being confined to home. She had plenty to consider and she enjoyed the break. Lying-in time was a rare opportunity for the usually busy mother to relax, collect her thoughts and contemplate life – as well as acquainting herself with her new baby. While she recovered from childbirth, Eliza spent many hours just gazing out across the estuary, quite content to do nothing more.

Lewis interrupted her musings and brought an end to the peace. He was feeling restive.

"Living in such an isolated, close-knit community is quite stifling Eliza." Lewis expressed his boredom with a sigh. "Do you think there is any chance we might escape again?"

"I'd rather not think about travelling at present," she told him before he put the suggestion to her.

"Lewis, you need to find a purpose in life. Can you not find something to occupy your time with?" Lewis grimaced at that.

11 The Travellers Return

"What did John Ayles say to your idea of setting up a wine dealership?"

"He wasn't impressed with the idea at all. He thought that becoming a wine merchant was beneath him. Your father, on the other hand," Lewis's frown turned to a lop-sided smile, "saw the merit of setting John up in such a business." John always seemed to be asking for financial support from his father-in-law. Seeing her husband was about to launch into a discussion of family politics, Eliza quickly ended the conversation.

With four children under the age of five in the household, days, weeks and months seem to run together for Eliza, immersed as she was in the trials and delights of pregnancy and motherhood. Stour Lodge was a home of satisfying mayhem and noise. Eliza rarely had time to reminisce about travelling, though she readily admitted to Lewis that she missed her forays into the markets of Lausanne. The cook and housekeeper took care of the domestic provisioning, so there was little necessity for her to venture out to the village.

Hers was the typical experience of the women she knew. The ideology of the time dictated that 'middle-class women were domestic creatures. They were concerned with home, children, and religion; they avoided politics, commerce and anything else which was part of the public sphere.'[4]

Lewis, meanwhile, tried hard to entertain himself. To escape the daytime domesticity, he entered wholeheartedly into the social activities of the local sailing fraternity, assisting John to organise the Walton Regatta in August 1832. He was delighted when Eliza took a break from her household activities to attend the regatta ball that summer at his side. Her parents and sister went too.[5]

He competed in the sailing races of the Harwich Regatta a month later.[6] That winter he even tried to enjoy the hunting and shooting pursuits of his in-laws. He went as far as to purchase an annual games licence at a cost of nearly four pounds. He also subscribed to various periodicals to inform better himself in the sport.[7] No matter what he tried, the lure of travel continued to plague his thoughts – and consequently Eliza's.

18 The Regatta, T. Alken

For the elite of England, travelling was a fashionable pursuit. It was certainly something that Lewis and Eliza enjoyed. Many well-to-do families tripped across the continent. Unsurprisingly, it wasn't long before Eliza and Lewis agreed that it was time to escape for a second time and another vacation abroad was planned.

In May 1833, an auctioneer was engaged. The boat and many of their household possessions were put up for sale.[8] They were preparing for a more permanent absence this time and the proceeds of the auction would help to finance their expedition. Once a respectable tenant was secured for the house, the family departed.

The family passed through Aachen, registering their arrival there in September 1833. There were five children in the party: Elizabeth Mary Ann, Vaudine, Lewis, Arthur and Rodolph, who was just out of long skirts. Eliza was busy preparing baby clothes again for she was midway into her fifth pregnancy by then.[9]

Mary Ann was born in Mannheim, Germany. The change of scenery did not alter much in Eliza's daily routine. She was just as

11 The Travellers Return

swamped by nappies and feeding routines as she had been at home. She was also teaching her elder sons to read and write. In the midst of juggling her daily responsibilities in a foreign country she received a devastating letter from her father.

My Dear Daughter,

You will be very sad to hear my news, indeed you cannot know how difficult it is for me to write this. Your beloved Grandfather passed away in his sleep last night. As you know he has been bravely suffering from various complaints for some time now, mostly the result of a good life well lived. However he broke his hip after a fall from his horse some weeks ago. Being bed-ridden was very hard for him and he suffered a great deal. It is better that he is no longer in pain.

Eliza was brought very low with the arrival of that news. She felt robbed of the opportunity to say goodbye to the venerable old man who had cared for her so much. Once the worst of her grief had abated, she was left feeling sad and angry.

"Grandfather's death means that Marianne will be mistress of Lawford House. Oh, she will be pleased. She has longed for that for years. I do hope she doesn't think she can dispose of the family portraits, she was always so critical of them."

Her anger against her stepmother surprised Lewis; the two had always been the best of friends, or so he thought. He shrugged his shoulders and concluded that his grieving wife just needed to find a vent for her feelings. Lewis had received a more business-like note from his father-in-law, with details of the will enclosed. He showed Eliza to reassure her.

"Don't worry, my dear. I'm sure she will not remove the portraits, your Grandfather expressly forbade that in his will."[10]

As it happened, Eliza did not have time to dwell on her sorrow for long. The family departed Mannheim later that year.[11]

They did not return to the Stour, however. Eliza was unwilling to face her family. There was reason to be embarrassed. Her husband had been in contact with his London lawyers to initiate a law suit against her father and uncle.

11 The Travellers Return

On Christmas Eve, 1834, the London papers announced the beginning of legal proceedings between Lewis, on the behalf of his daughter, and the trustees of her estate. His father-in-law, Thomas Nunn, was one of the executors of old Robert's legacy. Lewis had received information that there had been misappropriation of his daughter's inheritance. He took his concerns to the High Court, a serious undertaking for which he had to prove good cause. Several years passed before the situation was resolved.[12]

For the next two years the couple continued to travel. Their progress was interrupted by the birth of a fourth son, Thomas Griesdale in Tours, at the beginning of 1836.[13] For Eliza, as for most married women of the time, 'pregnancy might be hoped for or dreaded, but could rarely be planned or avoided.'[14]

By the time Victoria inherited the monarchy, in the middle of 1837, the family had returned to England. Victoria's coronation signified hope and expectation for the nation. Likewise, Eliza and Lewis saw it as a promise of progress and reform.

They made the decision to return to England, this time choosing to settle in the southwest. It was August 1837, when the couple presented their two youngest children, Thomas and Mary Ann, for baptism in Dawlish. When the local Vicar visited them soon after their arrival in the town, he suggested that such an occasion endorsed the family's establishment in the community.

Dawlish was a fashionable seaside resort where the mild climate of the south coast could be enjoyed. At the turn of the century, the marshy land near Dawlish's seashore had been drained for an extensive building project. Large mansion houses near the beach faced onto a manicured village green and pleasure gardens. Since the railway had not yet arrived, Dawlish was isolated, the preserve of local farmers, fishermen and the well-heeled.

The town boasted a lending library and public assembly rooms that were large enough to accommodate splendid balls. The Strand was the place to take the air, a place to meet with others and to be seen. Social activities were frequent and well attended by the more elite inhabitants of Dawlish.

11 The Travellers Return

In the warmer weather, sea bathing made a popular outdoor pursuit. There was a pretty, secluded beach set aside for the exclusive use of gentlemen. Lewis took the opportunities of summer to teach his sons to swim.

A magnificent structure on the main beach, the Bath House provided an enclosed environment for bathing. If Eliza wished to take to the sea, she would climb into a bathing machine, that is, a beach hut on wheels. Donkeys towed the trailers down the sand into the water. Ladies changed inside the hut and ventured out for their plunge by climbing down stairs straight into the water with the assistance of designated dipping women. Most importantly, modesty was preserved.

19 The Bath House on the Beach at Dawlish

Under the shelter of towering red sandstone cliffs, the beach provided the young Agassiz lads with hours of entertainment digging in the sand. Dawlish afforded plenty of open space to play ball and run. The ideal situation for a young family, Dawlish was a place where they could enjoy a civilised, yet healthy life style.

11 The Travellers Return

Lewis again purchased a yacht, which he named the *Black Eagle*, and participated in the annual summer sailing regattas.[15]

The births of more children followed: Frederic Carrington Agassiz was born in January 1838, then Alfred in 1840.

Eliza had given birth to eight healthy children, within twelve years. She was thirty-three years old. How she and Lewis counted their blessings.

Then, unexpectedly, tragedy struck. Little Thomas came down with scarlet fever within days of Alfred's birth. Lewis could not permit his wife to attend their suffering youngster, deeming her and the new-born at risk of infection.[16] Thomas had just turned four when he died.

Racked with remorse at being separated from her child, Eliza was inconsolable in her grief. Her milk dried up and a wet nurse had to be employed, for the first time in their marriage. Lewis had never seen Eliza brought so low and his concern for her over-rode his own grief.

Pride set aside, Lewis took Eliza back to her family in Essex. It was clear that the breach in the clan needed to be healed.

Elizabeth Mary Ann celebrated her twenty-first birthday that year in Bradfield, just a few minutes' walk from Stour Lodge. Some of her mother's cousins attended the celebrations in the village. Lewis exerted a great deal of effort into making that day one to remember for his precious daughter. His generosity made the headlines.

Although Lewis was determined on reconciliation, Thomas Nunn and Marianne did not attend that celebration – at least not according to the journalist who reported the occasion.[17] A certain Captain Frederic Brandreth was present. He had become acquainted with the family through his uncle, the curate at Mistley.

A few days after the birthday gathering, kinfolk congregated at Mistley Church. Frederic Carrington and Alfred were officially received into the family church at their baptism.[18] It was a significant occasion: the prodigals had been welcomed home.

Elizabeth Mary Ann was wedded to Captain Brandreth a short time later.[19]

20 A Fashionable Wedding, London Illustrated News

11 The Travellers Return

Lewis once again planned an elaborate event for his eldest daughter. Elizabeth Mary Ann's wedding at Mistley Church was not a small event, it was a fashionable affair. Afterwards, the 'elite of the neighbourhood partook of a splendid déjeuner' at Lawford House. Eliza was relieved that Thomas and Lewis appeared to be on speaking terms again.

Elizabeth's husband was a man that Eliza and Lewis had known for many years. He was trusted and admired, but that did not prevent Lewis from being anxious about his daughter long after the couple were seen off on their honeymoon. Eliza assured him repeatedly that Elizabeth Mary Ann would be safe in Brandreth's care.

Lewis needed a distraction. Nothing could be better to stop his worrying than planning a new adventure. The family's stay in Essex was not to last longer than the beginning of 1841.

12 Ach Tannenbaum

21 German Railway Station, 1841

'Rail Mania' had taken its grip throughout Britain and Europe. In the decade that had passed since their sixteen day epic across France to reach Switzerland, innovative engineering developments had revolutionised travel. Lewis's research revealed that the trip from London to Cologne could be achieved within thirty hours, by a combination of steamship and train travel.[1] Steamships departed from London on a Sunday morning, then arrived in Antwerp that evening. It took less than ten hours to travel down the Thames and across the North Sea. The train journey from Antwerp to Cologne occupied a further twenty hours.[2]

Despite the associated soot and grime, train travel appealed to Eliza. What greatly impressed Lewis was how much cheaper it was than road transport. Trains travelled faster than coaches did and additional luggage could be taken. Rail coaches were still very basic but even so they were much more comfortable for the passengers than bumping along uneven highways in a horse-drawn carriage.

In the early days of railway expansion, the Agassiz party had the use of their own separate compartment. There was no corridor to connect the individual cubicles, so privacy could be maintained. The children were able to make as much noise as they wanted, though Lewis tended to grouch if they were too loud. Eliza had a repertoire of songs and travelling games at the ready for restless youngsters. Whenever the train was scheduled for a stop, everyone alighted for refreshments in much the same way that they had previously at the, now old-fashioned, coaching inns.

Eliza's ninth child was safely delivered in Cologne, the principal city on the lower Rhine.[3] Lewis did not allow his family to stay there long. While Eliza was recuperating, he was out exploring the neighbourhood.

"My dear, the baby seems well enough. Are you able to travel again yet? You really must come and see what I've found." Lewis was enthusiastic about his latest discovery, but he wanted it to be a surprise. He had acquired a large house that he knew his wife would love. It was situated twenty-five miles further along the river from Cologne.[4]

"The distance isn't great by steamer and the voyage is tantalisingly scenic."

Eliza did not need convincing. Having read the Shelleys' account of their journey down that portion of the Rhine, she was pleased to climb aboard the steamer, baby and all, to enjoy the experience herself.

As Lewis promised, the river trip was not arduous. The children were all occupied on deck for the expedition. There was much to see. It was magical. Small towns, ruined castles, terraced vineyards and fortresses dotted the riverbanks. Eliza was not disappointed.

12 Ach Tannenbaum

> The part of the Rhine down which we now glided is that so beautifully described by Byron in his third canto of Childe Harold. ...We were carried down by a dangerously rapid current and saw on either side of us hills covered with vines and trees, craggy cliffs crowned by desolate towers and wooded islands where picturesque ruins peeped out from behind the foliage and cast the shadows of their forms on the troubled waters which distorted without deforming them. We heard the songs of the vintagers...[3]

When the boat pulled in at Königswinter, the family disembarked.

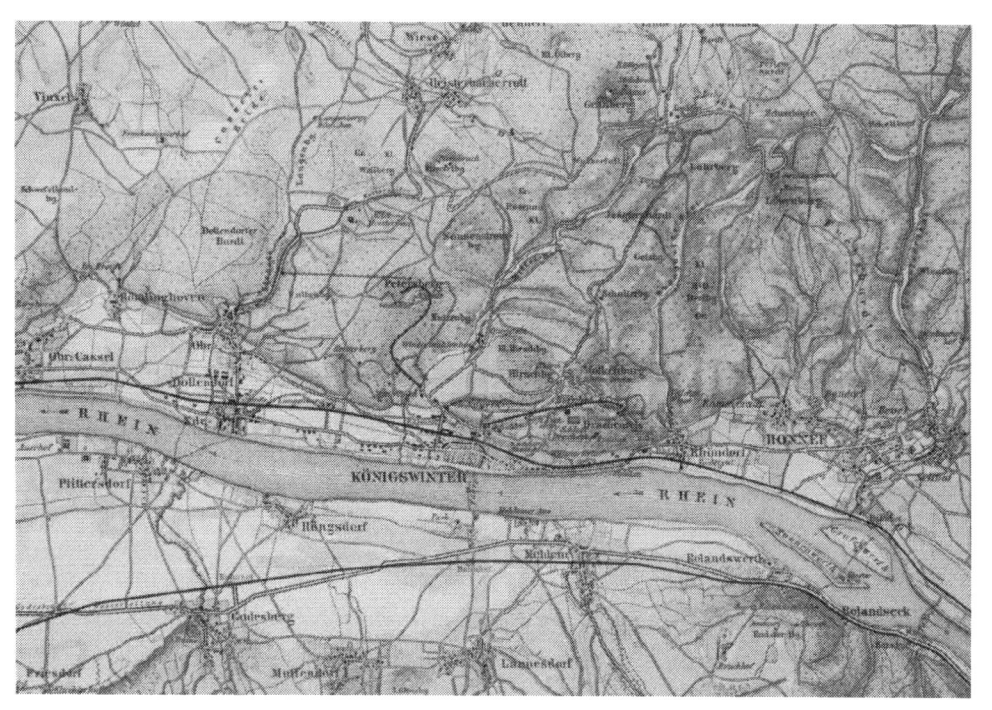

22 Map of Konigswinter

"The island on the opposite bank is Nonnenwerth, the Nun's Island. Rather fitting for you Eliza, a reminder of your roots." Eliza was busy feeding the baby – like his brothers, he was always hungry. She obediently glanced up to gaze across the water where her husband was pointing.

121

12 Ach Tannenbaum

"And the castle towering over it, that is called Rolandseck," Lewis continued. Eliza was still listening, though a little absentmindedly.

"Roland was one of Prince Charlemagne's warriors. Shakespeare's words went something like this I recall: 'Childe Roland to the dark tower came, His word was still Fie, foh, and fum, I smell the blood of a British man.' So here we are, British men at Roland's tower."[6]

"Roland. I like the sound of that. We'll call the baby Roland, Lewis."

The house that Lewis bought, on the outskirts of the town of Königswinter, was much more than simply a dwelling. It was an enormous villa with a turreted rooftop set in the midst of forty acres of vineyards and gardens.

"Oh Lewis, it's beautiful, it's a castle. Just like Grandmother Nicholson's house back in Lewisham."

Eliza had fond memories of that house. Her childhood dream had been of living in a castle, she knew her own children would love it. The strange language was not a problem for long. They all soon felt like they belonged to the district.

Christmas Eve dawned. The children expected a day of merriment and laughter, a day of treats. In the Rhineland, attending the Christmas markets was a seasonal highlight, a traditional family event. Everyone in the area gathered to visit the St Nikolausmarkt of Königswinter. The Agassiz family were keen to sample the delights of the market too.

The large party dislodged itself from the chaise in haste. Legs and bodies sprawled in all directions as the children tumbled out. They could hear music and laughter. Unable, at first, to see where it originated from, they were anxious to find the source.

Together, Mama, Papa, and seven children hurried along the street, around the corner. The baby was home with his nurse. They located their objective in the square in front of the Rathaus where cheerful sounds emanated from a group of red-nosed villagers.

O Tannenbaum, O Tannenbaum,
Wie treu sind deine Blätter!

12 Ach Tannenbaum

A crowd gathered around a loud, if a little tuneless, band of clarinets and horns. Heavy woollen cloaks and squashed felt caps outfitted the choir who carolled the merry melody. Feet tapped along with the big bass drum's booming rhythm. The resulting cacophony was accompanied by seemingly random, ear-ringing crashes of hand-held brass cymbals.

Eliza's children enthusiastically joined in with the singing. More delights were in store. Hints of vanilla, ginger, and cinnamon wafted across the square, mingling with the scent of warm bread. The wonderfully enticing aromas tickled their noses as they sang.

"Papa, Papa, I'm hungry," Arthur interrupted his father's wholehearted intonations.

"Eliza," her husband tapped her on the shoulder, "I think we're going to have to move along, the boys are starving." Still singing, she nodded gaily. She wasn't surprised. They were always hungry.

"Of course they are – who wouldn't be in this cold weather? Let's go boys!"

That was more than enough to set the boys scampering off to hunt out the source of the delicious smells.

Lewis Nunn and Arthur were thirteen and twelve. Between them, they had charge of their younger brothers, Rodolph and four year old Fred.

The little boys jingled the coins in their pockets with their chubby fingers, dumbfounded at the array of treats set out before them. They began sifting through the assortment of coloured sugar twists, *magenbrot* (gingerbread) and spicy *lebrucken* cookies. The *verkäufer* had a difficult task preventing the youngsters, as well as those who were old enough to know better, from sampling his entire selection.

Lewis and Eliza gave up endeavouring to keep the family together. Such attempts were unnecessary. Alfred was nearly two and hated being separated from his older brothers. His piercing wails sounded a reliable alarm if any of them should wander off too far.

"Here you are Papa, the girls and I have important shopping to do. We'll join you again shortly."

123

Eliza off-loaded the child on her hip to Lewis and took hold of her daughters, one in each hand. Eliza left her boys to make their culinary choices. She was pleased to have the opportunity to give her daughters a new experience, quite apart from enjoying the hustle and bustle of the markets. There was a tug on her arm.

"Mama, Mama, look at the dolls." The little wooden figurines in traditional costumes had Vaudine and Mary Ann mesmerised.

"Vaudine, please don't point. Oh I see. They're beautiful aren't they? Which one appeals the most?"

"I like the one in the red dress. Look she has a cape that's just like mine. Mama, she is so pretty. May I have her, please?"

"You have your pin money to spend, but are you sure you would rather a doll than sweets. You know the boys won't be sharing theirs."

While the girls were distracted by the intricate details of a miniature carved farmhouse kitchen, Eliza stopped to look at Christmas decorations. Planning a surprise for the children that evening, she was seeking the finishing touches. There were plenty of baubles to choose from. Hand-crafted wax ornaments, strings of beads, silver tinsel and glass balls vied for her attention, all carefully placed in baskets of straw. Eliza made her purchases.

When she looked back, Eliza was relieved to see Lewis had settled himself on a perch juggling a pewter tankard of *cierpunsch* in one hand, with Alfred on the other arm. He looked happy. She waved, and then she and the girls continued their browsing. They stopped to admire the carved biscuit moulds and nut crackers.

"Girls, don't let me forget to buy some oranges."

"And some apples Mama, look they are still so rosy and crisp."

Eliza was intrigued by the vast array of Christmas spices. She took the opportunity to make a few purchases from her list – more last minute Christmas preparations.

Later that evening, when Eliza was ready, she sent Lewis to fetch the children. He crept upstairs to the nursery door then rang a little bell. What a commotion ensued in response to that sound! The youngsters had been waiting for such a call.

"It's *Christkindl*, he's come!"

Six children in their nightgowns and caps immediately charged downstairs. Little Alfred was left wailing behind them. In Germany, the Christ-child appeared on Christmas Eve to leave gifts but only for well-behaved children of course.

As a body, they launched themselves into the drawing room. What caught the children's eyes were not the prettily wrapped presents, though there were definitely plenty there. The glistening fir tree towered above them. The fine silver tinsel and wire ornaments sparkled in the glow of what appeared, to the awestruck children, to be hundreds of candles. Glass baubles basked in the light adding to the effect. Delicately quilled snowflakes were Eliza's finishing touches.

"Fröhe weihnachten!" "Ein gesegnetes Weihnachtsfest!" Lewis shouted in delight, he was as much surprised as his children.

"It's a Christmas tree! Our very own Christmas tree," squealed Vaudine. She grabbed her little sister's hand and around they danced.

"Careful! Careful girls, slow down. We don't want to upset the candles!" Their father exerted himself to regain paternal decorum.

"Don't worry and fret so much my dear!" was their indulgent mother's response.

"Let's have some carols, Eliza." She dutifully settled herself at the pianoforte and began to play.

"A German one, first: *Stille nacht, heilige nacht.* We heard it this morning in the square, it's the King's favourite, so I hear."

Despite the small differences of language and culture, Eliza's life continued in much the same way as it had in Bradfield. Her duties were similar in Dawlish, Tours, Lausanne, or wherever her husband chose to establish the family.[7] Every day she had menus to write, servants to oversee, mending to be worked, laundry to be seen to, deliverymen to pay and supplies to be ordered.

The arrival of another daughter meant a new baby to feed. Eliza was responsible for the education of her younger children too, though her older sons attended a nearby school. If she had any

12 Ach Tannenbaum

spare time at all she would sit down at her writing desk and pen a letter to her sister.

What altered for Eliza with each new home was the view. Here, on the banks of the Rhine, Eliza looked out across the mountains every morning as she caught up on her needlework or instructed the children. On the edge of the Royal Siebengebirge Park, the craggy peak of Drachenfels, one of seven volcanic peaks, made a picturesque vista. Crowned by castle ruins, in legends it was the site of a dragon's cave.

23 The View from the Drachenfels

Lewis climbed to the top one morning, taking his eldest sons. He returned exhilarated, with a plan in his head. He could hardly wait to take the rest of the family.

"You really must see it Eliza, the view from the summit has to be seen to be believed. I've worked out a way for you to climb the mountain."

12 Ach Tannenbaum

"How on earth do you imagine I would be able to manage it Lewis, in these skirts?"

"Don't worry there are donkeys to hire for the purpose. You and the girls will be transported up. We'll have a family expedition. It'll be fun. We'll pack a picnic supper, cook it over a campfire, sleep in tents and have breakfast admiring the sunrise!" The dawn view from the Drachenfels summit was well recommended in the guidebooks of the day.

"Well I can't leave Eleanor until she's weaned or were you proposing she come too?"

"Why not, you'll take her on the donkey and I'll carry Roland on my back. Vaudine can take Alfred up onto her donkey if he straggles."

Situated as it was on the edge of the royal reserve, there was plenty of adventure to be had for them all. Lewis had chosen a home with a remarkable outlook and opportunity for outdoor pursuits. As well as climbing the many nearby peaks, Eliza's sons had space to learn to hunt game, fish and ride their horses.

The stony clay soil meant that the district's predominant industry was viniculture. The warm microclimate that had brought the family to Königswinter, made the perfect environment for cultivating white grapes, sheltered as it was by the surrounding Siebengebirge Mountains. Riesling was the most popular variety grown. Having had his interest piqued by the endless vineyards that surrounded Lausanne, during his visit to Switzerland, Lewis now had the opportunity to investigate the pursuit further. The possibility of sending German wine to England was simplified by the rapidly developing transportation methods of the day and his brother-in-law, John Ayles, was more amenable to the idea of a wine dealership than he had been a decade before.[a]

It made sense to leave the day-to-day running of his vineyard in the hands of the experienced local vintners. There were more pressing things to occupy Lewis. Eliza's castle needed to be bigger in order to house their ever-growing family. While Lewis redesigned their home, Eliza worked on the extensive gardens in her spare time.

12 Ach Tannenbaum

Though the community on the Rhine was small, it was not dissimilar to Bradfield. The Agassiz family were not lacking in company. Like every destination that Lewis and Eliza settled in, there were English acquaintances; friends, connections and sometimes even relatives. Königswinter and Bad Honnef were no exception.

There were dances every Sunday afternoon.[9] In the surrounding villages, all classes of people turned out in their best clothes, for the music. Everyone attended church in the morning first. Afterwards, even the most strictly protestant family's joined in. Eliza and all their children were happy to participate in the custom, it would have been rude not to. Lewis was a little hesitant. Such a frivolous activity as dancing was in conflict with his strict notions of Sunday propriety – he had first noticed the practice in Switzerland.

Towards the end of winter of 1844, Frederic Brandreth's brother arrived in Königswinter. The Reverend William Harper Brandreth, being experienced in pastoral care, had been requested to be the bearer of bad tidings.[10]

He delivered a tragic account - a message that their son-in-law had been reluctant to send by post. Elizabeth Mary Ann was dead.[11] She had died after the birth of her second child. The news was a terrible shock. This time, Lewis needed to be consoled over the unbearable loss of a child. Death due to childbed fever was an all too common misfortune. Eliza had delivered her children so easily that the dangers of childbirth were something that she and Lewis had forgotten. They had never considered that childbirth would threaten the lives of their daughters.

"I can't understand how this happened. Surely Brandreth thought to engage a qualified man to care for her." Lewis searched hard to find an explanation for the tragedy.

"I'm sure Frederic insisted on a physician being in attendance, his father being a medical man himself. You know these things happen."

"They don't happen to us. And where is he now, young Frederic, why could he not tell me himself?"

"Frederic will be a wreck Lewis. He has two infants to care for and his career to think of. Besides, he sent his brother for a reason. William will hold a special memorial service for us."

"Memorial Service! What would I want with that! I want my daughter, alive and healthy, and caring for my grandchildren."

"William says the observance will help Lewis. It's a chance to say goodbye."

Fortunately, family life continued to supply Lewis with many distractions. James Albert was born later that year.[12] At his christening in 1845, the names of the King of Prussia were added to the names his parents had chosen for him. Friedrich Wilhelm James Albert had the privilege of claiming the King of Prussia as his godfather. Lewis held a great respect for the King of Prussia.[13]

The sojourn on the Rhine ended a year later. They had lived in the castle for five years but there was a good reason for leaving.[14] Europe was in a state of turmoil. The King of Prussia was struggling to maintain peace in a nation beset by talk of revolution. When the initial disturbances began in 1845, the king had tried to repress the revolutionaries by utilising his armed forces. That strategy had worsened the country's unrest.[15]

The furniture and other family effects arrived in Harwich in the August of 1846 by sea.[16] This time, upon their return, there were clear and visible alterations to the valley.

The view across the estuary, one that Eliza and Lewis remembered with nostalgic longing, was in the throes of being destroyed – all in the name of progress. Eliza was not surprised when it prompted a temper display from Lewis. Somehow he held Eliza, or at least her relatives, to blame.

"What was your cousin thinking, allowing this to happen? Look Eliza! Look at the mess they are making down there. I can't bear to see such wanton destruction! They must be stopped."

Below Stour Lodge they could see an extensive disarray of machinery and men. It was a construction site. Deep muddy ruts scarred the grassy meadows and piles of wooden sleepers were strewn at random intervals along the fields.

The railway line connecting Harwich to Colchester was due for completion in 1847. For Lewis and Eliza that meant there would soon be trains belching black smoke and steam between their drawing room and the tranquil view of the Stour. The line was built through the fields belonging to Nether Hall that ran along the riverside below the house.

"Mama, why is Papa making such a fuss over the railway line?" Arthur wanted to know. "Surely it's a great thing. It connects us to London in a few hours. We won't be stuck in this tiny village in the countryside now." Eliza's boys, as they approached manhood, were beginning to question their father's strong opinions and frequent explosions of wrath.

Progress had reached the isolated Stour Valley in more ways than just the railway. Lord Rivers who had inherited the Mistley Estate from his mother, daughter of the late Colonel Hale Rigby, sold his Mistley inheritance in 1844.

The subsequent spread in ownership of the village greatly altered the community dynamics.

More land was developed and new areas of residential housing appeared between Stour Lodge and Mistley. With the sale of their home next to the Thorn Inn, Eliza's sister Mary Ayles shifted to Dedham.

Closer to Stour Lodge, the village of Bradfield altered too. It expanded into a little township with an assortment of new enterprises. Blacksmiths, bakers and shoemakers now provided the necessities of life meaning there was less reason to travel further afield to Colchester.

Living at Stour Lodge again was an uncomfortable experience. It felt like being trapped in a box. Though it had expanded to now contain six bedrooms, Eliza's 'dolls' house' was full to capacity, more than full.

Within days of the family's arrival in the valley, it was clear that escape from the close confines of the house was essential for the men of the family. There was little chance of that for Eliza and her daughters.

Eliza's eldest son, Lewis Nunn settled on a career in the forces. With a purchased commission in the Welsh Fusiliers, he sailed with his regiment to the Caribbean in 1847.[17]

Aged seventeen, and finished with schooling, Arthur considered himself a man. He took his Uncle Tom's suggestion, despite his father's warnings, and signed up for a gaming licence that winter, keen to participate in the country pursuits of his Nunn forebears.[18] Lewis had suggested he matriculate but Arthur was unsure just what career path to choose.

Rodolph worked conscientiously at his studies. He attended the local grammar school, as he aspired towards a university position. He also had the responsibility for his younger brother, Frederic Carrington. Fred was not so diligent and frequently exasperated his older brother with his classroom misdemeanours.

Alas for Eliza, now aged forty, she was expecting again and quite restricted to home. Vaudine and Mary Ann assisted her with educating the younger ones. Alfred and Roland both required supervision at their lessons. She also needed their help with the care of Eleanor, now four and Friedrich Wilhelm aged two.

Lewis, some thirteen years older than his wife, was beginning to slow down, his interests becoming more sedate. He frequently found the excuse to drive out in his phaeton, becoming embroiled in the business of the neighbourhood. One organisation, which took his time, was the local Provident Association that cared for the needs of the community's workers. He attended regular meetings along with the Nunn's and various other neighbours.[19]

The birth of another son stretched Eliza's nerves, Lewis's temper and the house's capacity quite beyond limits.[20] Stour Lodge was advertised to let and the contents of their house were advertised for auction.[21] The family vacated by Michaelmas 1849.[22]

They were on the move again.

13 The Matron

Exeter was 260 miles from Bradfield – two days travel by rail, with a stop in London overnight. The city was refined, a nice place to settle. With a population of thirty thousand, it was not overly large. Such a moderate size meant that the disease, poverty and pollution of the industrial cities were largely absent. To Eliza and Lewis that gave it an advantage over the ever-expanding metropolis of London. In 1849, it was well supplied with the urban amenities that they had become accustomed to on the continent.

Exeter was proud of its facilities and buildings. There were various assembly rooms and public promenades, tea gardens, educational institutions and theatres. A canal connected the city to the coast, enabling Exeter to function as an overseas trade port, with important connections to Newfoundland and Greenland.[1]

Eliza's new home was located in a genteel neighbourhood, not far from the cathedral and within a short walk to the shops. Nine four-storied mansions made up the attractive terrace of Colleton Crescent.[2] All of them overlooked the Exe and enjoyed the panoramic view beyond the canal across meadows towards the hills.[3]

The new abode, situated at Number 2 Colleton Crescent, was ideal for entertaining. It had huge formal rooms. On the ground floor were the dining and morning rooms where Eliza received her visitors. After dinner, the company would ascend to the first floor, ladies to the drawing room and men to Lewis's library. There were seven bedrooms to accommodate the family. Additionally, in the basement, the large kitchens and cellars provided ample space for more servants than Eliza had ever employed previously.

13 The Matron

The house was luxurious. It was fortunate for Eliza that the house was so lovely. She discovered that she was carrying her thirteenth child within a few months of the move. Once again she was confined indoors, unable to frequent the gathering places of the city, unable to visit the few new acquaintances she had made when they first arrived. She endeavoured to look forward to another confinement.

"A new house, a new baby," she told herself. Eliza adopted the affirmative maxim, in an attempt to keep an optimistic outlook. In that era, procreation was the core of a woman's existence; her purpose in life. Eliza's philosophy was no different. Her large family was a source of great pride. It was her crowning glory and earned her veneration and respect.

To have given birth to twelve healthy offspring was something of an accomplishment. Even then, families larger than eight or nine children were uncommon. Eliza knew too that she was approaching the end of her childbearing years.

Eliza's previous experiences of childbirth had been straight forward events so the difficult delivery took her by surprise. Elizabeth Ann's birth was followed by an unusually slow recovery for Eliza.‘ The time it took to regain her strength vexed her immensely, robbing her of the contentedness of her younger days. Instead, guilt was a constant companion as she rested. Her daughters learned to run the household in her stead.

Lewis made matters worse. He was in the midst of planning a trip to Canada with Arthur and Rodolph. He was anxious to depart, though he postponed the trip until he was sure Eliza was well enough to leave. With their departure looming, Eliza's mood sank lower. In her misery, Eliza began to sense that she was being deserted by her menfolk. Lewis had rarely left her side in their years of marriage.

"Now you're being melodramatic Eliza, of course he's not abandoning you," she admonished herself.

"Tomorrow they will begin their journey and it's your responsibility to see they are sent off in a robust state of mind." Eliza took control of her thoughts as best she could.

13 The Matron

"Lewis doesn't need the added complication of worrying about his wife while he's away."

She fleetingly wondered if Lewis was deliberately planning the separation, to avoid another pregnancy. After the complicated birth of her daughter, the doctor suggested it would be very wise to avoid the risk of another child. Contraception or the possibility of it had never been spoken of in her marriage. There were methods available, but they not for the use of respectable folk, nor were they reliable.

"Please don't be late tonight. I'd appreciate you being home to dress for dinner no later than five, Lewis," she told him over breakfast that morning. "It will be our last family meal for a while. I want it to be special. Your parents are arriving in time to dine at six." Eliza's father-in-law and his wife Jane lived on the other side of Exeter in St Sidwell's Parish.[5]

"I'll warrant you they grumbled about the lateness of the meal." The old naval commander was approaching eighty. Being somewhat old-fashioned, James John Charles Agassiz was used to dining much earlier, and was rather set in his ways. Lewis was not pleased at having to entertain his father. Their meetings never went well. While living nearer to him had been part of the appeal of residing in Exeter, sometimes it was a mixed blessing having them so close.

"Your brother and Louisa should arrive this afternoon in plenty of time, I've asked them to be early. They said they'll be here to take tea, when the boys get home from school."[6] Eliza found it prudent to have additional visitors when her father-in-law was present. If Lewis and his father ended up alone together, an argument invariably ensued. The presence of James David had a profoundly calming influence on the pair.

"Are you going to be able to get along, Eliza? With my stepmother, I mean. She is so critical. I know her sharpness upsets you." It was not only the old man that caused problems. Jane Agassiz, James John's third wife, enjoyed her role as family matriarch.[7] She was quite formidable and very prone to censuring the children for the smallest offense.[8]

13 The Matron

"I am getting used to her, really Lewis, I am," she assured him.

"Having Louisa here will make it easier to suffer Mother's complaints. Please don't fuss. It's important to see you fellows off with a cheerful family meal. Let's make the most of the evening." She realised that, given the choice, Lewis would have preferred to avoid the necessity of visitors on their last evening together.

"You don't think it is too soon to be entertaining again do you? You've been quite unusually teary lately." Lewis's tone was concerned.

She was a little disconcerted that he noticed how low she was feeling. Eliza could see that he was starting to consider remaining at home. However this morning she wanted him out of the house, so she was quick to reassure her husband that everything was in hand. "I'll manage. The girls are a wonderful help. Could you see the boys off to school please? Nurse will have them ready soon."[9]

It was going to be a busy day and Eliza was very, very grateful she had her daughters to relieve her of the bulk of the responsibility. Eleanor, though only eight, was already quite motherly. The little girl would gladly help Nurse take care of her younger siblings.

The girls all showed the results of having been taught well. Eliza was proud of their accomplishments. Vaudine would supervise the kitchen and make sure the dining room was arranged properly. Mary Ann always took charge of the flowers and wiping the glasses. Eliza had never trusted her servants with her prize possessions.

Really all Eliza had to do was feed the baby. That sounded easier than it was in reality. Baby Elizabeth was a poorly, fretful child. She always seemed to have a cold and had difficulty breathing. Consequently, nursing her was a long laborious process. That took the large part of Eliza's day.

The boys lurched through the door from school in high spirits.[10] They were pleased to see Uncle James. Their tired mother saw her sons for long enough to realise that they were all in desperate need of a wash and change of clothes before their grandmother arrived to inspect them. To her great relief Nurse managed that monumental task admirably.

13 The Matron

The remainder of the visitors arrived as planned. The children became quite subdued, and were very relieved to be sent upstairs after greeting their grandparents. Pinching was always an annoying threat when the old couple were about. However, it was the prickly, pointed questions that made them feel most awkward.

At six o'clock precisely, the dinner gong sounded. Lewis escorted his stepmother to the dining room.

They were dining *à la française*. For a family dinner such as this, the food was laid out on the table before the diners were seated.

Mary Ann's flower arrangement took centre stage. She had carefully kept the display low so that it did not disturb any conversation across the table. Vaudine had checked the napkins were clean and freshly pressed. She arranged the candlesticks to accentuate the flowers. There were oil lamps scattered about the room, but a dinner without candlelight was difficult to contemplate.

Eliza seated herself at one end of the table with the soup tureen and proceeded to ladle it out into the bowls at her side.

"Mulligatawny soup, is it?" Jane sniffed. "You don't think May's a bit late in the season for that Eliza?"

"Now, Mother, I know you feel the cold so I thought this would warm you up!" Eliza knew it was Jane's favourite soup despite the tone of her voice.

Lewis was dealing with the fish at the other end of the table. Jane turned to him and demanded, "Well Lewis. Are you not going to offer me wine?" He raised an eyebrow and cleared his throat. How like his stepmother to flout convention and not wait to be invited to partake of a glass. Although it was a family meal, it was rude of her to ask. Lewis could not help himself suggesting so, "I thought perhaps you might like to wait for the beef Mother?"

The old lady was momentarily speechless at her stepson's insolence. James David took her pause as the opportunity to change the subject. Searching for a suitable topic, he began by addressing the view.

"I can see why you chose this house Lewis, such a panorama to behold there across the river. If it weren't for the Haldons, I believe

13 The Matron

you'd have a view of Dawlish. Then you'd be able to see me working the vegetable patch."

Evening, however, was closing in and the view from the dining room was fading into darkness. A new topic of conversation was required. James David turned to Lewis Nunn, seated across the table.

"So Nephew, your battalion will be off again soon?"

"Yes we're based down in Plymouth at present but it will be back to Montreal for us later this year Uncle. This will be my farewell leave before we set sail." Though he knew his Uncle was interested in hearing more of his exploits, the young Lieutenant was unwilling to enlarge further on his occupation in front of his mother. That discussion could wait until the women withdrew.[12]

"I am so looking forward to our trip to Canada. It's been too long since our last expedition," Arthur began, only to be interrupted by his father.

"Speaking of which, Canada is a country that brings back memories for me. Do you remember our time in Canada when you were a child, James?" Lewis, the former midshipman, prompted his brother to recall their shared adventures on *HMS Rattler* as boys. "You were so young at the time. So was I really."[13]

The maid cleared the remaining fish, the soup tureen and plates, replacing them with the remove dishes that had been keeping warm on the sideboard. Lewis began carving.

"I just remember how cold it was, not much else," was James David's reply.

"Ah yes, those were fine days," his elderly father interrupted suddenly. The *Rattler* was held up in Newfoundland for the long icy winters. I enjoyed those extended visits. Such gay society – the ladies – they were uncommonly handsome I seem to recall – they were accommodating and friendly too, there was one in particular with whom I..."

"Captain!" Jane interrupted before her husband forgot himself. "We'll have none of that talk, your granddaughters are present!"

It was Louisa's turn to step into the breach this time.

13 The Matron

"Eliza, while Lewis and the boys are away next month, I was thinking you might like to come to visit for a few days. You could attend our archery club with us. I hear you were once quite the toxophilite."[14]

"Why yes, I have always enjoyed a little archery but I've not been able to indulge much since we were married. I'm not really sure that I can leave baby Elizabeth just yet. We will have to see if she settles a bit better."

"And you can save the baby talk for later thank you Eliza!"

Old Jane could not resist butting in again. Being childless herself, Jane deplored any mention of the problems of motherhood.[15] Eliza refrained from responding, she had to concede that it was not a subject for the dinner table.

Arthur brought up the forthcoming journey again. "Father has booked us passage on a lumber boat – can you believe that?" It was a safe subject to discuss. Everyone had something to say about the trip.

"They make the return trip to Prince Edward Island without much cargo, so the captains try for as many passengers as they can muster, to turn an extra profit. I can't imagine it will be comfortable. No doubt it was the cheapest passage available."[16]

"Well Arthur, you can hardly blame Father for that, since the purpose of the expedition is for your benefit." Rodolph was to accompany his brother. He was having second thoughts on pursuing a scholarly career and his parents thought that a break from his studies would help him mature.

"It will be a capital adventure; I can just see the pair of us managing a plough. What a lark!"

Though her eldest son remained at home to support her in his father's absence, Eliza bore the weight of family responsibilities. Vaudine at twenty was a good assistant. However, in addition to her and Mary Ann, there remained six school-aged children and the baby to care for.

What complicated life most of all for Eliza was that Elizabeth Ann was not well. The baby's frailty was more obvious every day.

13 The Matron

Lewis returned from the journey to Prince Edward Island a few months later. He was satisfied with his purchase of a farm for his sons. Having taken the trouble to equip it with the necessary tools, Lewis assured Eliza that her boys were secure and safe.[17]

"Yes, they will have to face the trials of the harsh winter but farming will toughen them up and give them purpose in life," their father reported optimistically. "It's quite a substantial farm, Eliza but I engaged plenty of workers to see them through the harvest."

"I do worry about them being too isolated."

Eliza's baby died of a chest infection just after her father's return. She was buried in the Dawlish churchyard alongside her brother Thomas.[18]

That was not the only tragedy to strike the family, for less than a year later Eliza and Lewis heard with a shock that Arthur had perished in an accident on the island.[19] When Rodolph returned home, he was quite broken, his self-confidence destroyed by the loss of his older brother. Caring for her son was a distraction from Eliza's own grief.

Frederic Carrington missed his elder brothers. Though he was eight years younger than Arthur was, Fred had worshipped both his oldest brothers, particularly Arthur.

Arthur had always looked after him. He and Lewis Nunn had taken Fred on adventures: camping trips, pheasant hunting, and fishing. They had taught him to swim and to use a gun. Rodolph had returned but Rodolph was not the same person he had been before the farming episode. He offered no companionship for the youth.

Fred lay on his cot on the fourth floor of his father's house. That was the only space he could call his own, in a room he shared with his brother. Bored with school, the brooding adolescent dreamed of escape. He hated living in the city.

The situation was aggravated by his father's reaction to some of his exploits. His attempts at finding urban adventures for himself had resulted in misconduct. His father suffered the public humiliation of having one of his sons hauled before the mayor when Fred was accused of smashing some street lamps.[20]

24 Coming Home, W. Morris

Worse, the local newspapers reported the case in disparaging terms. Lewis's fury was unimaginable.

Eliza wrote to her sister recounting the tale.

> *What shall I do, dear sister? My husband is beside himself, torn between shame and wrath. Unfortunately, they are of a similar nature, though I would never dare say as much. I am relieved that Frederic has not come downstairs for a meal since it happened, since his father cannot bear to see him. I can see he's bored with school and he appears uninterested in further education (just like his father). We need to find the lad a position. Louisa has suggested that some time at sea might be the solution perhaps. Would you see if there is anything your John might suggest?*[21]

Mary refrained from responding that Fred was as like his mother, as he was like his father. She pursued the matter of what to do with Fred and a position was found for him. Frederic Carrington left school and went to sea.[22]

Lewis Nunn settled with his regiment in Canada. He had not been there long before he wrote home to announce his engagement to a Miss Caroline Schram. He asked that his father purchase him a new army commission because his lieutenancy would not provide sufficient income for him to support a wife on.[23]

Lewis flatly refused. His angry response surprised Eliza for hitherto Lewis had been an indulgent father; he took his responsibilities for providing for his family very seriously.

By the time Lewis relented and agreed to the commission, his son had resigned his post in the army.[24] With the farm on Prince Edward Island sitting unoccupied, it made sense to transfer the ownership of it to the newly-weds. Eliza's first grandchild was born there the following year.[25]

Lewis was no longer the energetic, fun-loving companion he had been. He launched himself into church politics upon the family's arrival in Exeter.[26]

The speeches at public meetings and petitions continued after

13 The Matron

Lewis returned from Prince Edward Island. He spent long hours in heated debates and then came home and railed against the evil he believed was threatening his evangelical faith. He wrote many letters to the local newspapers expressing his feelings. Eliza decided that it was better to stay out of his way some days. His passion was something Eliza struggled to understand. She did not address that subject with her sister.

Keeping in contact with her sister was vitally important to Eliza. There were many subjects, which Eliza could only confide to Mary. In some ways, the sisters found it was easier to share in writing: their worries and fears, their delights and joys. Still, Eliza missed her sister's companionship. It had become especially so in the last few years.

In their letters, Eliza and Mary Ann discussed the intimate subjects they could talk to no one else about. The average age of menopause at that time was forty-five.[27] They were both approaching what their contemporaries called the 'evening of life'.

The end of the childbearing years was akin to the onset of old age for a Victorian woman. Life altered substantially. Both social and recreational activities became more limited. Only serious pursuits were deemed suitable for a woman over forty-five. Novel reading was too frivolous an activity for a Victorian matron. Likewise dancing was unseemly. There was a belief that a woman of this age was more susceptible to over-excitement if she engaged in these activities. That would threaten her mental health. Even attending the theatre was frowned upon.

It was acceptable for Eliza to act as chaperone for her daughters however. If they were ever to find husbands, it was essential that Vaudine and Mary Ann be seen at societal functions. Lewis now avoided such engagements if he could. Fortunately, the Royal Subscription Rooms, where such public assemblies were held, were close to their home, opposite the New London Inn.

When Louisa Ayles visited the Exeter household in spring, Eliza wrote to her sister again, this time to report on her niece's vacation.[28]

13 The Matron

> *It is delightful to have your beautiful daughter to visit. She certainly seems to be enjoying herself, making the most of all the city has to offer a young woman. The girls have been studying the fashion magazines together and reading of the latest hooped underskirts.*
>
> *Today they went to the High Street, in search of the trivial things that girls hold so dear. I saw them set out on their walk with pleasure, thinking them such a fetching group.*
>
> *I suspect their corsets were tighter than usual – for they all seemed to have diminished in size overnight.*
>
> *It reminds me of when we were young. How we used to fuss over our bonnets, always pulling them apart to add a new adornment or ribbon. I believe Louisa will report to you herself how much she enjoyed the ball at the Subscription Rooms.*

Mary Ann was swift in her reply:

> *You made brief mention of hoops. I have seen them in the magazines also. What do you think of those silly new crinolines sister? I know I do not approve of them. The wide skirts seem rather awkward, they are always jiggling and bumping around. They must be rather draughty around the legs too.*
>
> *I would prefer it if you could persuade Louisa out of purchasing one please. They are not for my daughter. I'm sure this fashion won't last long when ladies realise how ridiculous it is.*

Eliza could not help but nod her head in agreement with her sister's sentiment.

14 The Mourners

Thomas Nunn's health was failing by the time that Lewis and Eliza returned to Stour Lodge in 1856. He died the following spring.

The sisters held vigil at his bedside together, watching their father fade away over his last few days. They took turns to cool his forehead and dampen his lips. He knew his daughters were there and it pleased him. Marianne had been relieved to relinquish the task; she needed a rest from nursing him.[1]

Now Thomas's body was washed and he was laid out in his best suit and a new white shirt. Flowers and candles filled the morning room at Lawford House. Thomas Nunn looked at peace. His three eldest children could hear folk gathering in the next room.

Thomas Nunn was an important personage in Manningtree having served the community as both magistrate and banker for the past forty years. Friends and relatives had come to pay their final respects and were waiting for their opportunity to do so.

Mary held Eliza's hand as the siblings said goodbye to their father. Their brother Thomas rested a hand on each of their shoulders and gazed down at the old man pillowed on white satin.

"Poor Father, how hard we tried him at times."

"My husband took him to court."

"Mine owed him thousands of pounds."[2]

"He never blamed us for those things though. Though he was strict, he was always fair, we always knew he would be reasonable when we were children and later as adults too."

"Do you think he felt crowded by all the women in his life? Marianne and her girls made great demands of him."

14 The Mourners

"We all made demands of him Mary. It was fortunate he had Uncle Carrington constantly beside him. And he had you too, Tom. You were always his pride and joy."

"I don't believe Uncle Carrington has left Father's side for more than an hour at a time in the last few weeks."

"He'll need your support today. Losing his brother will be hard on him."

After the last mourners filed out of the room, the family were alone again. The minister said a few words. Then the undertaker stepped forward to secure the coffin. Thomas's son and grandson were pallbearers. His sons-in-law, John Ayles, Richard Nicholl and Lewis, joined them. Carrington was there too. The weathered old man was only two years younger than his brother was.

Thomas Nunn's coffin was placed in the hearse with the care and respect he deserved. The four, plumed horses led by the customary mutes, made slow, dignified progress down the road, towards the churchyard where he was to be buried.

Thomas's will declared his intent to leave Lawford House and his banking concerns to his son, Eliza's brother, Tom. The remainder of his estate, valued at over thirty thousand pounds in its entirety, was to be divided between Eliza and her three sisters.[3]

Lewis's father died later the same year in Exeter.[4] James John Charles Agassiz mentioned Lewis in his will too but only to complain that his son had failed to repay an outstanding loan.[5]

Eliza was still wearing her mourning crapes when tragedy struck again the following year.

Her brother suffered an 'untimely and melancholy end'. His horse bolted and caused his dogcart to overturn.[6] Young Tom, now aged 54, was found insensible on the road. He died a few hours later.

A funeral cortege wound its way from Lawford House once more, four mourning coaches making the procession. Tom's son – Eliza's nephew – Thomas William, and his Uncle Carrington were the chief mourners. The deceased's brothers-in-law followed them: John, Richard and Lewis.

14 The Mourners

Lewis and Eliza celebrated their thirty-first wedding anniversary in 1858. As their elder sons reached adulthood, the nomadic upbringing that Lewis and Eliza had provided them with, influenced the way the boys sought to establish independent lives.

There was another factor that affected their sons' choices. England was undergoing a migration period of epic proportions as modern transport options opened the possibilities of new horizons all over the world. There were opportunities to be had by the adventurous and those who were willing to bear pioneering discomforts. Gold was the topic of the day.

Lewis Nunn, aged thirty, succumbed to gold fever in 1858. He left his wife and three children in Ontario, in the care of his parents-in-law, to journey to the other side of Canada on his own. It was three years before his wife joined him in Victoria, British Columbia. His mining venture being unsuccessful, they headed up river from Victoria to Hope where he took a job as the postmaster.

Rodolph was also in Canada at that time. His eldest daughter, Maude, was born there in 1858. Rodolph had married Mrs Mary Blackett (née Shafto) the previous year. When they returned to England, Rodolph decided to return to Cambridge to study theology. He was twenty-seven. Lewis purchased the living of Great Clacton, a village 12 miles to the south of Bradfield, to secure future employment for his cleric son.

Roland joined the Royal Marines as a gentleman cadet shortly after the move to Essex. By 1861 he was gazetted as First Lieutenant. He lived on board various vessels as his duties required. He made the voyage to Malacca in 1862, but most of the time was based out of Woolwich.[7] He regularly returned home to spend his leave in Bradfield.

After working aboard several passages to the antipodes, Frederic Carrington took discharge from Green's Shipping in 1858. Time spent with his eldest brother influenced him to seek his fortune in the gold mines of America.[8] He dispatched the occasional, brief letter to his mother, enough to let her know he was alive. She would have liked to have known he was happy too. Fred joined the

14 The Mourners

American Union's forces that were gathered in Red River, New Mexico in 1860.[9] America was facing Civil War.

Alfred was closest to Fred in age but rather more studious. He matriculated and attended university to study medicine. Later, after being admitted to the Royal College of Surgeons he vanished off to the distant and wild frontiers of New Zealand.[10]

The rest of the family settled down to a quieter life at Stour Lodge.[11] The three daughters, Vaudine, Mary Ann and Eleanor remained at home in Essex along with their youngest brothers, Friedrich Wilhelm and Edward Albert. The boys attended Dedham Grammar School.[12]

Eliza and Mary were no longer confined to written communication. They enjoyed having the leisure to spend afternoons together, chatting about their families and gossiping about the neighbourhood.

Though Eliza was hesitant when the idea was first suggested, she and Mary collaborated to manage the relationship between Vaudine and John Mount Ayles between them. Vaudine married John at Bradfield Church in 1861.[13]

That same year, Lewis bought a farm on Bradfield Heath. It was an investment opportunity that he would have been unwise to have ignored, but Lewis was not a farmer. Lewis spent many more hours in his study working on his notes than he did overseeing his farm. He had it in the hands of a bailiff until one of his sons was prepared to take on its management.

There was a gap in Eliza's life now. Previously, there had always been children around to entertain or educate. She only had two sons living at home. Her daughters were well able to take care of themselves and their own wardrobes. Eliza found she was able to return to her long-since forgotten paints and sketch books once more.

One afternoon in July, Lewis was ensconced in his study as usual. Seated at her easel in the drawing room, Eliza squinted out across the estuary, trying to catch the hazy effect of the afternoon light on the water. She would have preferred to paint out of doors but that

14 The Mourners

summer had settled into a weather pattern that was miserable and wet.

Suddenly a loud noise jolted her out of her seat.

"What on earth was that?" Lewis thumped his book down with a bang and bellowed to his wife from the library. "What are you up to Eliza? I told you not to disturb me!"

Eliza still had a brush in her hand as she swept outside onto the terrace. The noise had come from further down the hill, nearer the beach.

"Something's happened Lewis, all I can see is smoke. It looks like something terrible has happened." She pointed across the fields with her best sable as he hobbled out to her, leaning on his stick.

"What are you looking at? I can't see anything."

"Look down there, along the railway line. There's been an accident. See the dust and smoke? It's clearing a little so you can see people moving about now. It doesn't look good. Something terrible has happened," she repeated again, standing on her tip toes with her hand shading her eyes. "It looks like the train has been derailed. Oh my, look, the carriages are all tumbled over."

"I knew it! I knew it was going to happen sooner or later. Those tracks are in a terrible state of repair. I've informed the railway company several times."[14]

"Lewis, we must go down there," Eliza interrupted her husband's ramblings. "They need help."

"Yes Eliza, I agree. Off you go now and take Ellen with you. You need to find out what's happened for me!" Eleanor and Eliza set off towards Bradfield in the dog cart, as soon as the groom brought it around.

"We'll go to the vicarage. Margaret's bound to know what it is that's happened." Margaret Hayle was the Rector's wife, a close friend of Eliza's.[15] Situated a quarter of a mile from Stour Lodge, it only took a few minutes to convey the mother and daughter to the Bradfield Rectory.

"Eliza, thank goodness you've come. There's been a terrible accident down on the line."

14 The Mourners

"We heard the noise from home. The crash sounded horrific."

"The train toppled off the rails just before the station. They're bringing the passengers here."

"Was anyone injured? There must be fatalities."

"Oh there has been word of a few minor cuts and bruises. We'll be able to deal with some of those ourselves but there are medical men on their way just in case. There's only been one fatality that I've heard of so far. The stoker was killed outright. There are many women and children down there, all quite distressed, poor things."[16]

"So we'll need lots of hot, sweet tea. Off you go to the kitchen Ellen, see what you can do to help there."

"Cook is already working on that and the parlour maid is setting trays as we speak. Most of the passengers just arrived at Harwich on the Rotterdam steamer. Some are German as well as Dutch. I don't speak any foreign languages myself but now you're here, communicating won't be a problem. You and Ellen will take care of talking to them won't you? I know you both speak German at least. It's good you've come to help Eliza."

25 The Illustrated London News, July 23 1864

15 The Widow

The curtains were drawn. Stour Lodge looked like a house put to sleep. Inside, the mirrors were covered and the clocks stopped. Black crape and ribbons were draped across the front door. The wreath on the gate at the roadside signified to passers-by that Lewis Agassiz was dead. Stour Lodge was in mourning. The inhabitants of Mistley and Manningtree knew and so did those of Bradfield.[1]

Eliza had been worried about her husband for some time. His health had deteriorated over the past few months. She wrote to her children of her concerns, but there was no more she could do.[2]

The day had begun well enough. It was a cheerful spring morning. The sun was shining. When Eliza and Ellen returned from a walk through the fields, they paused outside the front door to admire the wisteria on the south-facing wall. It was Eliza's favourite time of year.

All was quiet when they entered the house, ominously quiet. Lewis did not answer when she called. Eliza's heart skipped a beat when she found him in his chair slumped over his desk. The first thing she did was to right the inkpot that had emptied its contents over the Turkish rug on the floor. Then she called her daughters.

There were formalities to follow. The physician confirmed what they could see themselves. He stopped by at the vicarage on his way home to notify the Rector. Margaret hastened as soon as she heard his report. She knew Eliza well enough to send her husband to fetch Rodolph from Great Clacton to take charge of the situation. The groom was dispatched to Dedham to notify Mary. Rodolph arrived as soon as he could extract himself from parish duties.

15 The Widow

"Eliza, we need to contact your boys. Mary Ann, do you know where they are?" The Ayles arrived within an hour of Rodolph.

"Friedrich and Edward went to Colchester for the day, they should be home soon."

"Oh dear, they will get a shock when they arrive, perhaps someone should be on the lookout for them at the gate," Mary suggested thoughtfully. Then she continued working through a mental list of Eliza's offspring.

"I know Roland is at sea, so he can't be reached until they put into port. Both Lewis Nunn and Fred are across the Atlantic aren't they?"

"Yes Aunt Mary. We can send a message by telegraph to Hope for Lew but we have no contact with Fred at present, he could be on his way home, he could be anywhere! The last word we received from him was that he was planning to leave his regiment." Eleanor's tone of voice sounded her anxiety for all to hear.

"It's alright. I will write to them this evening, a letter from me will be better than a telegram." Eliza spoke softly, soothingly to her daughter. "There's no need for any urgency. Hopefully the army will forward it on to Fred if they have an address for him."

She had been quietly sitting in the background behind all the commotion. They had forgotten she was there. Eliza was dignified, outwardly calm. Inside her heart was in turmoil but Eliza knew the etiquette to adopt for such a time. She took a deep breath and began to follow the protocols that would carry them through the difficult days ahead. It was best to keep busy. There was much to be seen to and decisions needed to be made.

The undertaker had already delivered the lead-lined coffin that Lewis had chosen some time ago. The man was standing by his cart outside, awaiting further instructions. It was not his place to intrude.

"Mary Ann, could you make out an order for the crapes, please, and Eleanor, we need to get the cards prepared."

"Is there a text you prefer for them, Mother?" That was an urgent decision for the cards needed to be printed, as soon as possible, for distribution.

15 The Widow

"Just work on the list of recipients for now and then we'll discuss it over tea. Try not to forget anyone." Mourning cards notified the neighbourhood of the forthcoming funeral arrangements.

Eliza stood up and made for the door. She turned to her sister. "Mary, would you help me lay him out now, I'd like to do that myself, rather than letting a stranger do it."

Alone with her sister, Eliza felt she could be herself. "I can't believe this has happened. He was well and in fine voice this morning when we left him here in his study. He wanted the house in silence so that he could concentrate." Her voice faltered. Lewis's death was a shock, even though she was aware of his declining vigour. She had been his wife for 39 of her 60 years. A future without her life's companion was difficult, if not impossible, for her to contemplate.

Eliza's nerves were a little restored after she had seen to her husband. It had been soothing to wash his body, gently, slowly, quietly – in the tranquillity of his library, then to bind him and re-clothe him in the new shirt she had just finished stitching. Her sister stood beside her – as she had when they laid out their Father together.

Rodolph, having spoken to the undertaker of his mother's wishes, hovered nearby in case they needed his help with any lifting, but he was careful not to interrupt the ladies' work. Like the undertaker, he knew it was best to wait quietly.

Later, Eliza settled at her desk to write. The letters to her sons were more difficult to compose than she anticipated. She had hoped for over a decade now that Fred would come home in time to make peace with his Father. That was no longer possible.

"I've been thinking about the black edge on the cards, how thick should we have it Rodolph?"

"Enough, but not extreme – a quarter inch should be sufficient Mother. Everyone holds Papa in great enough respect: we have no need to be crudely explicit in our grief. That would be common."

"I agree, nevertheless make sure you speak to the undertaker about good quality black gloves and crape for the mourners,

15 The Widow

Rodolph. It's important to show your Father the veneration he deserves."

When the funeral director returned the next morning, Rodolph and John dealt with him, giving instructions for decent ostrich feather plumes for the horses and staffs for the mutes who would lead them. He would provide crape armbands and gloves for the mourners. There were many trappings required for a respectable Victorian funeral.

Mary and John stayed in the house for the next few days. There to receive callers, they ensured the family were not disturbed. Vaudine also remained with her three little ones and Eliza took solace in having her grandchildren around her.

Rodolph's large family were in Great Clacton with their mother. There was a new baby in the house so Eliza's daughter-in-law was unable to venture out.

Eliza's mourning clothes arrived without delay. Being readily available meant there was little choice to be had in the design of first crapes. The heavy black fabric of Eliza's dress had a matte finish. The lively sheen of a regular silk was unsuitable for grief. Indoors she wore a widow's cap. For outdoors, there was a bombazine mantel to wear against the chill and a bonnet with a black veil. Her neckline was furnished with a broad weeper collar. After the burial, white weepers and cuffs would be worn, but for now, they were black.

Less than five years had passed since Victoria's Consort, Prince Albert, had suffered a premature death. That was in 1861. Being in the public eye, the distraught royal widow had set an example for future mourners to follow. According to custom, Eliza was not expected to leave the house for twelve months. If she did venture out, it would only be to attend church and her face would be suitably veiled. Whereas Queen Victoria chose to remain in widows' weeds for the rest of her life, it was acceptable for Eliza to discard the black crape after two years, when she went into half mourning.

Eliza and her daughters said farewell to Lewis in their home. Only the menfolk attended the burial service.

15 The Widow

The legal ramifications of her loss then needed to be addressed without delay. When Lewis wrote his will, he expected that Eliza would be cared for by her offspring. He determined that her marriage settlement was to be divided amongst the children, and the life insurance that he took out at the onset of their marriage for her protection, was directed by his will, to be bestowed elsewhere. He bequeathed their home, the six acres it stood upon, the pictures and the furniture of Stour Lodge in quarter shares between Eliza and their three daughters. Though she was named as his Residuary Legatee, the advowson occupied by Rodolph, was the only possession Lewis left in her hands.

The will would not have caused problems if their daughters had all remained single. When Lewis died, Mary Ann and Eleanor were still spinsters, but Vaudine was married.

John Mount Ayles, Eliza's nephew and son-in-law, notified her in writing that he was anxious to receive his wife's share of the inheritance within days of Lewis's death.[3] Unruffled, she accepted the terms of the will, satisfied that she could help the young couple. However, it was not a simple transaction. Long discussions were held with Eliza's solicitors and they decided that the house must be valued and transferred into a trust to fulfil the terms of the will. Eliza then gave a quarter of the assessed value of the house and land to Vaudine's husband.

John Ayles reluctantly agreed to wait for a special valuation of Lewis's pictures. A settlement on those was delayed for some time. Lewis owned a valuable collection of art, which he bequeathed in equal shares to his womenfolk.

Friedrich Wilhelm took the opportunity to make his claim on the estate too. His mother obliged by paying him his third share of Street Farm. He also sold the stock which his father had left him.[4]

Eliza's youngest sons remained at home with their mother. They still ventured out for social events that year, not being under the same mourning restrictions as their womenfolk. Friedrich and Edward, now 21 and 19, returned to their old school to enjoy the Dedham Grammar School athletic sports.

15 The Widow

Edward was blind by then and dependent on his brother. He had lost his sight while attending a military college. His handicap did not prevent the fellows attending a ball in Dedham later in the year.[5]

26 Mary Anointing the Feet of Jesus by Rubens

16 The Grandmother

Family matters continued to occupy Eliza. There was not much time to dwell on her loss. She would not have wished it any other way.

"Of course we'll attend the service Rodolph. I couldn't miss the celebration. Your father was enthusiastic about the refurbishment at Great Clacton. It's such a shame he didn't live to see the completion of it." Rodolph's success was significant to his mother. She wanted to show him her support. It was more important, in the absence of his father, for her to do so.

"You must tell me what we can do to help."

The eight-foot thick walls of the Church of St John in Great Clacton were crumbling when Lewis bought the living. The ramparts were constructed in Norman times. The decayed state of the church did not deter the family or Rodolph's new congregation. They adopted an enthusiastic restoration plan. The building began as soon as he and his family were settled into the vicarage.

Eliza and Lewis gave all the encouragement and support they could to their son's project by helping to raise the funds required. A reputable architect and builder were engaged and under their supervision the old plaster crust that covered the walls was removed, the stonework repaired, buttresses rebuilt and a fresh tile floor laid. The high boarded pews were replaced with the more modern bench pews at the same time. The final cost of the repairs was £1100.

The local congregation, as well as the Agassiz's neighbours and friends, from Bradfield and Mistley, contributed. Colonel Brandreth, now bearing the surname Gandy, kindly donated towards the work.[1] So did her nephew, the banker, Thomas William Nunn.

16 The Grandmother

Eliza and her unmarried daughters took specific responsibility for funding the brass pulpit desk. They paid for the restoration of the font, the refurbishing of the communion table, and the tiles for the pediment upon which it stood.

A service to celebrate the completion of the repairs was conducted by the Bishop of Rochester on 7 December 1866, less than eight months after Eliza was widowed. Since it was a religious event, it was acceptable for her to attend the auspicious occasion.

The Rector of Bradfield, accompanied by his wife Margaret, pulled into the drive early that winter's morning to collect Eliza. The girls were to catch the train as they could not all comfortably fit in the Rector's carriage. It was a faster journey by rail, but not as convenient. Not with all the provisions they had packed for the luncheon event.

Eliza was concerned that too much work might be expected of her daughter-in-law at the vicarage. Mary Isabella had her hands full managing her little ones, without the additional stress of providing a luncheon for the Bishop. Consequently, with the aid of her friend Margaret, and her daughters, Eliza intended to take charge of the midday meal that was to be provided for the celebration's attendees.

By the time the service was due to begin, the women had the tables laid out and the seating arranged to their satisfaction in the school hall next door to the church. They pulled off their aprons, set their bonnets straight and hurried into the church just in time for the processional hymn. Having dutifully listened to the readings and the sermon, the ladies scurried out before the end of the service to make sure the maids had finished warming the food.

"Well that was a rather lovely service I think Margaret. The children's choir were surprisingly tuneful. Rodolph fretted a great deal over whether they would be ready for the event. He had trouble getting them all to attend the extra rehearsals he wanted to hold outside the regular school hours."

"The dulcet tones of children's voices do make an occasion special, but it is a very difficult performance to accomplish in a small village. He did a grand job with the local children." Margaret

16 The Grandmother

scooped tea leaves into the biggest teapot she could find while Eliza filled the sugar bowls.

"The Bishop's sermon was superb, fitting for the occasion. He looked satisfied with what the parish has achieved here."

"I'm sure you must be very proud of Rodolph. That new surplice he was wearing, was that one you've made Eliza? I know you were working on his chasuble and some stoles too."

"Embroidering those was a great privilege for me. I wanted them to be worthy of service to God."

"The congregation won't be much longer. It's freezing out there, they'll be glad to come inside." While they oversaw the last minute preparations, the Bishop was directed outside the church to consecrate a piece of land that had been added to the churchyard.

"Are we almost done Eliza?"

"Yes, I think we are ready. Thank you for your help. Maud could you fetch a maid to stoke up the fire, please?" Eliza's granddaughter had been with her all day helping as she was able.

The day was reportedly a great success.[2]

Naturally, the responsibility for his mother and sisters fell to Rodolph since he lived in the neighbourhood. Nevertheless, he was unsure whether his mother's visits to the Great Clacton vicarage were more help or hindrance for his harried wife. Mary Ann and Eleanor took the trouble to assure their brother that the outings were a great comfort to Eliza.

"She doesn't entertain much these days Rodolph. Really the only times she ventures out of the house are to call on Aunt Mary in Dedham or to go down to you. It's good she can catch the train to Clacton, it makes the trip very convenient." Mary Ann was the more sensible of the daughters; she could see how important it was for her mother to retain some sense of independence.

"Mother loves spending time with your little daughters, Rodolph. She really seems to sparkle when they are about. She appreciates having something vital to do."

"Watching her with them reminds me of the close times we had with her when we were girls," Eleanor added.

16 The Grandmother

"Now that you mention it, I have noticed that she has been teaching them to stitch. My dear wife is gratified for that since she has so little time herself to take up fine work, let alone the patience to teach our oldest two daughters."

"You know how Mother enjoys fine needlework, Rodolph. Passing on her skills seems to have become quite a passion."

27 Very good; Very good indeed!

Eliza took pleasure in overseeing the girls' handiwork and taught them to darn socks as well as to stitch a dainty seam. "Now girls, take a careful look at what I am doing. A good darn needs to be as

16 The Grandmother

invisible as possible. It must be comfortable to wear so it should be soft, not hard and lumpy.

"Father complains that his old stockings give him blisters Granny. Mama seems to have trouble getting the darns right."

"That's because your mother has too many other things to see to Maude. It's time you were able to help her. Look at this repair work. Your father shouldn't complain about this darn rubbing his heel. See how even it is. Now get to work, the mending basket is overflowing so you'll get plenty of practice."

Rodolph's youngest daughter, Frances Eliza, was still an infant. She had been born just before Lewis died. Rodolph had three little sons in addition to his three daughters. Sometimes, when he had business nearby, Rodolph brought the children to Stour Lodge to visit her. They all loved to play on Lewis's lawn and frequently fought over the old swing in the garden. Eliza sat outdoors to watch the girls play on the seesaw. She regretted, wistfully, that Lewis was not there to enjoy their company.

"How Lewis would have enjoyed such days," Eliza remarked to her sister one afternoon. "Those boys of Rodolph's need a grandfather to teach them to sail and to fish. Their father never seems to have time for such matters."

On 7 February, ten months after the death of Lewis, Eliza's daughter Vaudine died, leaving four tiny children without a mother. Fanny, the youngest, was only a few weeks old. Vaudine's death was a stark reminder of the perils of childbirth.

Vaudine's name was added beneath her father's on the marble memorial that was installed in Bradfield Church. Vaudine and her father had been close. She and her infants had spent much time with her parents in Essex, her children being born at Bradfield while her husband was at sea.[3]

There was a further rupture in Eliza's life when John Mount Ayles remarried.[4] Having had the care of Vaudine's children for a year, the marriage effectively removed them from Eliza's sphere of influence. Vaudine and her children were not the only family members that Eliza missed.

With her sons living overseas and married to strangers, correspondence again became her solace. Relying on the post was the only way Eliza was to ever know her Canadian grandchildren but that did not make them any less important to her. Hearing of the struggles the family faced in Canada prompted her to send them parcels: she shipped out side saddles for her granddaughters so that they could ride. There was a croquet set sent too as well as clothing.

The Canadian family had lived in the Fraser Valley, near Vancouver, in British Columbia since the beginning of the decade.[5] Eliza read accounts of the family's activities in letters she received from Florence, her eldest grand-daughter. The young lady penned long descriptions of their lifestyle to her English grandmother. Eliza found those quite entertaining though she did wonder why her daughter-in-law Caroline put up with the hardships and scrapes that Lewis Nunn subjected her to.

Lewis Nunn Agassiz was a large man. He stood some six foot two inches in height, and, according to his daughter, he 'did not know the meaning of the word, fear.'[6] 1867 was the year that burly Lewis Nunn moved his family to Ferny Coombe from Hope. According to Florence, Lewis Nunn refused to pay the cost of shifting his family by boat. Instead, he improvised, constructing a raft that was made up of two Indian canoes joined by planks. Florence wrote that 'he loaded household belongings, chickens, and children – everything on it.'[7]

Eliza commented to her sister, "Caroline bears much more than I ever had to. I thought those expeditions across France were adventure enough. But this account makes my anxiety over keeping my babes in clean smalls seem quite insignificant. Listen Mary."

> *Father, who was an expert in a canoe or a boat, took command. He was in the stern of one boat and there was an Indian in the other, two squaws paddling in the bows. The other Indians helped where necessary.*
>
> *How we ever kept the children from falling overboard I do not know. Dick was only two years old and determined to cast himself into the foaming waters.*[8]

16 The Grandmother

"It seems he inherited his father's taste for adventure, Eliza."

"Oh yes, he was always like his father, but far less cautious. My little Lew was very headstrong. It doesn't appear that he's changed much."

Eliza laid the letter in her lap and pulled her handkerchief from her pocket. Giving in to misery was not something she often indulged in.

"Eliza?" Eliza pulled herself together and passed the letter to Mary, "You really must read this account."

"Florence writes entertainingly doesn't she? Do you think she exaggerates? Oh my, she writes of wolves, blizzards, mosquitoes and forest fires. How unbearable it all sounds. You're right; her mother must be a very strong woman to cope in the face of such hazards."

"Florence also tells me that with her mother so busy, she takes all the responsibility for stitching the family's clothing herself. I gather there are no local shops or seamstresses. It must be very make-do. How hard they all work."

"How old is she Eliza? From her letter, Florence appears very grown up and resourceful."

"Florence is only thirteen. I must send her some of Eleanor's cast offs. There's a good pink silk that has only been worn a few times. I doubt Florence has ever worn silk.

"What about a sewing machine Eliza? Can you imagine how useful that would be out in the wilds of British Columbia?"

"That's a marvellous idea, Mary. Yes, I shall do that. I saw one in the catalogues the other day that would be perfect, a hand machine. It was small but looked quite robust enough to send overseas."

"Have you heard from Frederic Carrington Eliza?"

"I did receive a short letter from him, some time ago. He left the army and married last year. He and his wife Ellen have a son now, William his name is. I do find it sad that I have so many grandchildren that I will probably never meet."

1867 was the year that Roland married.[9]

That Christmas her daughters and grandchildren decorated the house. Eliza watched them at work with bunches of holly and

16 The Grandmother

boughs of fir that they had collected from the woods. The soft smile on her face reflected her peaceful heart.

28 Christmas Time by Miss E. Osbourne, 1865

16 The Grandmother

"Are you feeling alright Mother?"

"Yes, I'm quite well, I was just remembering other years. I have so many memories of Christmas's past."

"Happy memories?"

"Only happy memories Ellen, I've had a fortunate life."

"Where shall I hang the mistletoe? Over Father's precious Ruben's do you think?" Ellen asked with a mischievous smile.[10]

"Oh Ellen, it's just a copy."

"I realise that Mary Ann, but Father loved it so much. Do you think he appreciated the way Rubens depicted the place of a woman?"

Eliza was still lost in her thoughts, but her daughters were well used to the old lady's reminiscing.

"Times have changed so much since I was a girl. Mistletoe was something only the servants used to decorate the kitchen. It provided plenty of entertainment down there. We never used it amongst the trimmings in my father's house, respectable people didn't do so. That is until the Christmas your father came to visit."

"What happened then?"

"Oh, you know, it was just a bit of fun," Eliza's voice cracked a little but she smiled up at her daughter.

Within a short time, it was proper for Eleanor and Mary Ann to enjoy a resumption of their social life. Edward and Friedrich escorted their sisters, the Misses Agassiz, to parties and local balls.[11] Sometimes Eleanor entertained friends and family with her skills at the pianoforte. She performed at a concert in Great Bentley in early 1869.[12]

After a few years, Eliza also laid aside some of the restrictions of mourning. Though Eliza followed the Queen's lead, she also paid attention to the fashion magazines. Resolving not to appear dowdy, she replaced the crapes in her wardrobe with new rustling silks. There were a few subdued colours added to her wardrobe but her dresses were still predominantly black. She wore delicate collars and cuffs that she hand-worked herself to match her indoor caps and lappets.

With the changes in fashion, skirts were no longer as full as they had been. The cumbersome crinolines, which, against their better judgement, both she and Mary had eventually succumbed to wearing, were finally disappearing. A narrower silhouette replaced the wide voluminous skirts of the 1860s. The new, pulled-back skirts were shaped by the *tournure* or bustle. The Punch magazine suggested the out-moded cage crinolines be used as plant protectors.

"Oh yes, the cucumbers would flourish underneath those steel monstrosities Eliza!" That thought made the old women laugh.

Eliza enjoyed taking up an active social life once again. She was not as energetic as she used to be, but appearing in public was unavoidable, for she still had unmarried daughters. They attended concerts, dinner parties and balls together. The Colchester Subscription Ball took place in the Town Hall in the spring of 1870. The guests arrived after nine in the evening then dancing continued until the early morning.[13] The Agassiz women attended without a male companion, by then all Eliza's sons had left home.

Edward was in Worcester attending the College for the Blind Sons of Gentlemen. Worcester was a long way away from home and Eliza missed her youngest son. Nevertheless, the college gave Edward unique opportunities to prepare for an independent life. It was a new establishment and Edward made the most of the facilities offered. He took singing lessons and excelled at swimming, winning first in the College swimming sports that year. The newspapers reported that he was such a strong swimmer he had rescued a man from the Thames – quite a feat for a young man with no sight.[14]

"I've taken a new appointment Mother. The curate will take charge at Great Clacton." Rodolph announced his intention to move his family to Leicestershire in 1870. Eliza had to be philosophical, despite her reliance on him. Rodolph had eight children of his own by then and there were his two older stepdaughters as well. They needed a much larger home than the Great Clacton living provided.

"I'm sure you'll be fine Mother. Mary Ann seems to have everything in hand. Besides, we'll be a little closer to Edward there. You will be able to visit him when you come to stay with us."

"Perhaps it's time we moved on also, Rodolph. With you gone, there's no reason to stay in Stour Lodge. I had a letter from your Uncle James. He isn't very well. He complains of dizzy spells, with intermittent palpitations and he has such trouble getting around. It sounds as if he is partially paralysed. He is lonely I expect. I think the girls and I might take a trip across to visit him for a time."

"Yes, I agree Mother. Some company might perk him up; I expect his home shows the signs of missing a woman's touch too."

"Nevertheless, I will miss you sorely. We must take the family to Colchester for some likenesses to be taken of you all. There's a new studio there which apparently does good work, it is well-spoken of."[15]

It was a decisive step to take but it was time to sell the family home. Eliza tried to rent it out first.[16] By the end of summer, 1870, it was sold.[17]

17 Old Age

Eliza and her two unattached daughters entertained few misgivings about departing Essex since there were clear advantages to the relocation. They were contented enough to establish themselves permanently in Devon.

Exmouth was known for its temperate climate and mild winters, frosts and snow being less frequent in the southwest. The weather was not the only benefit. With two miles of golden sandy beaches, Exmouth was a popular, bustling seaside resort. It enjoyed the appropriate amenities of a smart spa town. There were assembly rooms, lending libraries and public baths as well as a new promenade along the length of the beach. The town was lit by gas and had a good water supply. Exmouth was a healthy place to live. The fortunate inhabitants advertised a significantly lower mortality rate than that experienced by Londoners.

In addition there were the advantages of their new home. Compared to Stour Lodge, the mansion at Number 8 Louisa Terrace in Exmouth was splendidly appointed. Situated close to the shore in the fashionable part of town, it had a vinery and greenhouse, six bedrooms and three sitting rooms. The terrace faced south towards the sea, looking down across the Exmouth Beach Promenade. From the rear it looked north towards Exeter and the Haldon Hills. The outlook rivalled that of Stour Lodge. Eliza decided, very soon after her arrival, that she was not going to miss the old familiar views after all.

The main drawback of living in Devon was being so far from her sister again. Eliza had already departed Essex when she heard the news of her brother-in-law's death. She had to be content with

17 Old Age

offering Mary her condolences by post. She deeply regretted that she was not there in person to offer her support, however she accepted that Mary had her own sons and daughters and would be well cared for.[1]

James David Agassiz lived alone with his servants after the death of his wife, Louisa, in 1867.[2] He had suffered from severe gout and various heart problems for some years since.[3] The old man was grateful to have the company of his nieces and his sister-in-law.

29 Exmouth from Louisa Terrace

Eliza quickly took charge of their new home. She and her daughters busied themselves, sorting, cleaning and organising the accumulation of James' years of bachelorhood. New curtains were installed, the greenhouse restored, and the garden coaxed back to life. There was plenty to keep them all busy. Their presence took James David's mind off his miseries and filled the quiet empty spaces of his large luxurious home with life and feminine sparkle. As it happened, he did not enjoy their company for long.

James David Agassiz, died on 12 February 1871.[4] He bequeathed his home and furniture to Mary Ann, a sum of money to Roland and an allowance to Vaudine's children.[5] There were also various bequests for his wife's family.

17 Old Age

James David assigned his favourite nephew, Lewis Nunn Agassiz, £1000. When the isolated Canadian family heard the news of the inheritance, they were overcome. It was more wealth than they had ever known. Lewis Nunn soon put the money to sensible use, purchasing new equipment and a flock of sheep for his farm.

Being within twelve miles of Exeter, Eliza and her daughters lived close enough to visit Jane Agassiz and provide the old lady with some company.[6] There was time to mend their relationship before the older widow died in 1871, aged 90.[7]

The family benefited from Jane's will. Mary Ann received possession of her grandmother's china and her grandfather's epergne. Jane's farm in Burlescombe was bequeathed to Roland, Lewis Nunn, Mary Ann and Vaudine's children in four equal shares. Fifty pounds was Eleanor's portion but there was no mention of Eliza's other children; Frederic Carrington, Friedrich Wilhelm, Edward Albert or Rodolph.

The beach was only a few minutes' walk from the house. The promenade made a pleasant escape in the summer months – a place for picnics and donkey rides. Rodolph and his family visited so that the children could enjoy the seaside. Eliza was content to watch them as they dug in the sand and chased the gulls, splashed in the water and learned to swim. Though she felt herself too old for sea bathing, her daughters were brave enough to indulge in the healthy exercise. Exmouth was a happy place to live.

The recent deaths in the family circle did not bring the social life of Mrs and the Misses Agassiz to a complete halt as their father's death had. Although Eliza no longer looked forward to evening ventures as much as she had in her youth, her daughter's convinced her that it was important to be seen attending some functions. The Exmouth Imperial Hotel was only six minutes' walk from their home. It was a frequently used venue for balls. Attending the receptions there was a convenient way for the women to participate in the life of the community.

Friedrich escorted his mother and sisters to the Yeomanry Ball at the end of summer of 1871.[8]

30 Dressing for the Ball, The Graphic, 1870

What a commotion ensued in the house that evening. The maids were hard pressed to see to the demands of dressing the three women in time. Intricate hairdos with ringlets and curls were contrived with hot irons. Feathers, flowers and ribbons added to the effect of delicate coiffures. Even a widow such as Eliza enjoyed the frippery associated with an evening party. She liked to dress up. Therefore, dress up they did, their dresses covered with the pleats and flounces, ruching and frills that were in vogue.

The evening was warm, with a gentle breeze sweeping in across the sand: enough to refresh but not to disturb. The party-goers entered the foyer of the hotel, greeting their friends and neighbours. With everyone suitably attired for the auspicious occasion, it was a colourful gathering. The new synthetic dying processes had introduced brighter shades of colour into the Victorian fashion world. Magentas, violets and greens were the hues of choice that summer.

The large urns of fresh flowers that greeted the guests at the door, added to the rainbow effect.

Having discarded wraps and checked their hair, the ladies adjusted their long gloves, took up their fans and entered the ball room. There, the chandeliers twinkled and glistened in the candlelight, reflecting the kaleidoscope of colour.

"They've done a fine business of decorating the venue."

"It's breath-taking! And isn't it such a wonderful night for dancing?" Eleanor's fan was open and working as she gazed around the room. She was looking for a particular young man with whom she hoped to become better acquainted that evening.

"Can you see him, Ellen?" Her mother asked.

"Oh dear, am I that obvious?" Eleanor blushed, "He said he would be here."

"There he is, he's coming our way," Mary Ann nodded in Philip's direction.

"Good evening ladies, I'm so pleased to see you here. My, Mrs Agassiz you look elegant."

"Thank you for the compliment Mr Davies. Girls, I'll be off now, I have friends to speak to."

The scene brought back pleasant memories for Eliza. How she had loved these evenings as a young wife. Lewis had been a gallant dance partner. She missed her husband but not enough to prevent her enjoying herself.

After consuming an elaborate meal in the adjacent dining room, she sat out of the way of the swirling skirts with her neighbour, Mrs Waters.[9] Together they watched the youngsters and reminisced of occasions when they too had enjoyed such energetic waltzing.

"Eliza, I have noticed a young gentleman paying particular attention to your Ellen."

"I don't think Mr Davies has left her side all evening, I would be so pleased to see her married and settled. Don't you think Ellen is beautiful tonight?"

"I won't deny that Ellen is a beautiful woman. Nevertheless, in our day to encourage such focussed attention at a public gathering would have been frowned upon."

"Yes but we did all we could to inspire it didn't we Mrs Waters?"

Eleanor was in love. At the respectable age of thirty, she married Philip Davies, a stockbroker, at the parish church of Littleham.[10] The Reverend Southey, who had been husband to one of Eliza's half-sisters, travelled down from his parish at Kingsbury, Somerset to officiate at the ceremony.[11] This wedding was a cause for celebration in the family. Eliza was pleased to lavish all she could afford, to mark the occasion of her youngest daughter's marriage.

The following year, in 1873, the family enjoyed another wedding ceremony. This time it was the turn of Friedrich Wilhelm James Albert Agassiz. He married Julia Garnault in the neighbouring parish of Withycombe Raleigh.[12]

Eliza wrote some of the details of the wedding to her sister.

> *Dear Sister, I hope you are steadily recovering from your sad loss. Not that there can ever be a full recovery from the loss of one's partner in life. But we old women muddle along quite well without them I have found. You must be glad of the company of your daughters. I know I have always been grateful for the joys that my children and grandchildren bring. They are such a welcome distraction from the sorrows of life. We are so fortunate you and I. That reminds me to ask, have you any news of your son and our shared grandchildren?*
>
> *But I digress dear sister. I wanted to tell you about our happy occasion. I do not recall if I referred to Friedrich's planned nuptials in my last note to you. It was such an event for little Exmouth. The local newspapers made the most of it. They reported a 'gay and interesting' occasion. The father, of my newest daughter Jessie, was once a General in the Indian Army. She is beautiful of course, as you would imagine Friedrich's bride must be. She went to a great deal of trouble to deck herself out in the latest fashions. She was indeed as 'richly dressed,' as the papers reported.*

> *The service was followed by a splendid déjeuner afterwards at her family home. I have never seen the like. The couple set out immediately for Nova Scotia for their wedding holiday. I am anxiously awaiting news of their safe arrival there.*

Jessie and Friedrich's eldest daughter was born in Nova Scotia the following year.[13] They decided to stay in Canada. The births of two more children followed in Nova Scotia during the time that Friedrich attended university there. He was ordained in 1876.[14]

With Friedrich's departure from home and Eleanor busy tending her husband and new baby daughter, Eliza and Mary Ann might have felt the large house was empty. However, that was not to be.

Taking employment on a ship bound for home, Frederic Carrington made the journey from the United States. He was a broken man at the time. His wife had died and his two children were placed in care.[15]

"I can't face life without her. I blame myself for her death. I should have been a better husband to her." Eliza knew his grief was overwhelming but it was clear that there was more than grief tormenting him. Frederic Carrington was slow to reveal the source of his unhappiness. When he did begin to talk, Eliza was very attentive.

"You probably think I have abandoned my children."

"What has become of them Fred?"

"I've left them in an orphanage."

Eliza could not answer him. To desert one's children was something neither she nor her husband would ever have contemplated. Nevertheless, she was mother to this suffering man and could only treat him as such. Whatever else had transpired, Eliza was pleased to have him at home once more. It was nearly twenty years since she had seen him. She measured him up rather proudly. He was handsome. There was no arguing with that. Like her, he was fair and blue-eyed. When he left home as a gangly youth, she had hoped he still had some growing to do. However, Frederic Carrington was much shorter and leaner than his eldest brother. He measured five foot seven.[16]

17 Old Age

"She was of the Catholic faith, Mother. That's why I left the children. I promised Ellen that I would see them brought up in her faith. I couldn't see any other way that I could do that. I will never see my little ones again, but believe me, there was no choice."

Frederic looked up at his mother and held up his hands.

"Father would never have forgiven me if he had known that I married a Catholic girl!"

"Shush Fred, that's not important. Your father may well have surprised you on how he felt about it. He would have loved her for herself anyway."

"You know we called our little girl for you, Mama. Eliza is such a darling child, so pretty." Fred's agitation was clear in the way he tugged at his whiskers. "How could I leave them? Will they be alright without me?" Eliza reached out to her son, wanting to soothe him and set his troubled mind to rest.

"The important thing is that you know they'll be cared for. You'll be able to write to them. As you well know, penning letters is my only link to so many of my own children. For now, though you need to take time to rest and heal. Then you will have the chance to begin a new life. I know you are strong enough to take the opportunity, you've done so before."

The same year Eliza's eldest son answered her pleas and returned home to England to visit his mother.[17] Eliza was 'wild with joy and happiness' at seeing him. Despite leaving his wife and ten children on a remote farm in British Columbia, Lewis Nunn appeared to be in no hurry to return home.

Fred recovered from his losses, as his mother predicted. For him, Lewis Nunn's appearance gave him the opportunity to take leave of his family again, without suffering any pangs of guilt.

Knowing his mother was being cared for, Fred departed from London in the autumn of 1874, bound for New Zealand on the *Waitara*. It took 82 days for the ship to travel to the other side of the world before arriving in Lyttelton Harbour in November.[18]

Eliza never saw Fred again. She was pleased when he wrote to tell her of his marriage to Harriet a year after his departure.[19]

17 Old Age

It was crucial for her to know that each of her sons experienced the support and comfort of a reliable partner. She sat down with some fine white lawn and worked some dainty handkerchiefs for the new bride. It was only a trifle, but it was something that would post easily. She hoped her daughter-in-law would treasure the token and appreciate the time invested.[20]

Roland too visited his mother. He and his wife had just the one son, Thomas, born in 1870 in the first few years of their marriage. Roland did not seem happy when he came home on leave in 1874. He stayed a few doors from Eliza and Mary Ann in a house on Trefusis Terrace.

One evening, the lieutenant was found drunk in the streets of Exeter and was summoned before the magistrate to answer charges of violent assault. Roland confessed to a 'trifling obfuscation,' but claimed the violence was in self-defence. His brother-in-law, Philip Davies, supported him in this and Roland walked free on the payment of a fine of forty shillings.[21] The charge did not affect his career. Less than a year later, Roland was promoted to a captaincy in the Royal Marines.[22]

Life settled down to a pleasant rhythm. Much of Eliza's time was spent stitching clothes for her grandchildren. It was an absorbing task that provided her with a sense of purpose. She felt valued and needed by her family.

In addition to her needlework, Eliza continued to dispatch frequent epistles. She regularly wrote letters to her absent sons, her grandchildren – and to Mary. The sisters still scribbled long descriptions of the trivial amusements and frustrations of everyday life to one another as they had always done.

Mary's letters had become less frequent of late. Examining the few that did arrive, Eliza noticed Mary's handwriting was becoming uneven and shaky. It was no longer the daintily executed script that she and Mary had been taught by their governess as children. 1875 was the year that Eliza's sister died.[23] Mary's three unmarried daughters were still living with her in Dedham. Eliza wondered how they would manage. She would miss her correspondence with Mary.

17 Old Age

When Edward Albert married Maria Webley-Parry they enjoyed a society wedding. Since it was held in London, Eliza took rooms there for a few months, so that she could be present for the event.[34]

Edward's mother was proud of the way her blind son managed his disability. Though he could no longer engage in the physical pursuits that her able-bodied sons enjoyed as young men, losing his sight encouraged Edward to develop other talents. He and Maria shared a love of music. They frequently entertained at events with sung duets and piano recitals.[35] The couple settled in Exmouth where their only son was born in 1879. They resided very close to Louisa Terrace at a lodging house on The Beacon.

Lewis Nunn remained in England for longer than expected. He was still there in 1877 when he escorted his mother and sister to a subscription dance in Exeter. Mr and Mrs E. Agassiz also attended this occasion.[36]

When Lewis finally set off on the long journey back to British Columbia, he failed to complete the trip. He died tragically in Acre, Syria, of sunstroke on 16 June 1880.[37]

Having received the news of her eldest son's death, Eliza suffered further grief a few months later when her beautiful daughter Eleanor died.[38] Eleanor's children were tiny. The youngest, Rowland, was only three. He had two older sisters. Lillian was five years old and Nellie was aged six. Eliza and Mary Ann could not abandon these infants and made plans for their care.

They took residence in Whalley Villa, a house on Shooter's Hill Road, in Blackheath. The house was close to where Eliza's son-in-law, Philip Davies, lived. The move enabled them to contribute to the upbringing of Eleanor's children.[39]

With their seaside home no longer in use and the life in Exmouth abandoned, Mary Ann's house on Louisa Terrace and various family effects were advertised for auction.[30] Jane's old crown derby tea set was disposed of in the sale as were various valuable paintings.[31] Among other items included in the auction was a miniature donkey carriage that the ladies had used to venture forth to the beach.

178

17 Old Age

The move from a seaside resort to London's suburbs was not undertaken lightly; it effected a substantial alteration to their lifestyle. Still, Eliza enjoyed good health and had enough energy to assist with the children's care.

The fortitude and determination with which she had survived the disappointments and sorrows of the previous decade were waning, nonetheless. Growing weary of life, Eliza was feeling her age, but she refused to feel sorry for herself. She considered herself fortunate that she had a daughter to care for her. The unmarried Mary Ann was her only daughter who was still alive. Mary Ann was a very sensible woman.

For Eliza, the return to London signified a completed life circle. She had been born not far from Shooter's Hill. The ladies took a drive through Deptford one day, and up the hill towards Lewisham. A wall now surrounded Stone House and the old trees had grown gnarled and bent. It was difficult to see the house from the roadside. New residences surrounded it, crowding it out. Loam Pit Hill was no longer the open countryside of her childhood.

Eliza's final little jaunt, in a lifetime of travel, took place in the summer of 1882. Eliza and Mary Ann set off on vacation. Eliza was seventy-six at the time. That was a grand age to be taking a seaside holiday. They travelled south by rail to Portsmouth, where they stayed in Southsea.[32] Besides enjoying the seaside, there was another reason for their journey. Roland was stationed a few minutes' walk from their lodgings, at the Royal Marine Headquarters.[33]

Some months after the return to London, Eliza suffered a stroke which left her partially paralysed. On 30 March 1884 she passed away. There had been a sufficient time lapse, between the stroke and her death, for her children to gather to say their farewells. Roland was notified and was present when Eliza relinquished her hold on life.[34]

Eliza's body was transported back to Essex to be interred. She was buried alongside her husband and daughter Vaudine. The burial took place on 4 April, 1884, at the Church of St Lawrence, in Bradfield, Essex.[35]

179

18 The Memory

Of Eliza's fourteen children, (including her stepdaughter) she outlived seven.[1] Mary Ann, Rodolph, Friedrich, Edward and Roland, were the only children who remained living in England at the time of her own demise.

Eliza had installed a beautiful memorial plaque at Bradfield, after Lewis's death. Vaudine's name was inscribed on it the following year but Eleanor's was not. There was more than enough room for Eliza's name to be added to the marble monument in due course. For some reason, her children omitted to do so.

The blank space on the family memorial somehow suggests a sense of inconsequentiality to Eliza's life.

Yet, despite the restrictions that were placed upon women who lived in that era, Eliza's life was full and productive. She was a daughter, a sister and mother, as well as a wife, then a widow. She fulfilled her obligations as a neighbour, employer and parishioner in addition to her family roles. 'Nineteenth century women were remarkable both for the restrictions within which they operated and for all they achieved in spite of them.'[2]

Sarah Eliza was no exception. She was not insignificant. Nonetheless, as the archival records reveal, Eliza's life was lived in the shadow of her menfolk, first her father, then her husband and then her sons. She had no voice in the world apart from theirs to speak for her.

The reason for the glaring blank space on the tablet will never be known. Maybe there was a better use for the money it would have cost to have the engraving done. Eliza herself may have requested her name be omitted. Perhaps Rodolph, Friedrich, Edward and Roland decided their mother was not worthy of a memorial.

Perchance, there was no reason at all and they simply forgot. We will never know.

Sarah Eliza Agassiz was gone.

Illustrations

1 Sarah Eliza Agassiz 5
2 London seen from Blackfriars Bridge, 1814 15
3 Stone House. Used with the kind permission of Deptford Local History and Archives Centre 21
4 A Regency Ball Dress, Ackermann's Repository 28
5 The Cornfield by John Constable, engraving by A.W. Penrose, 1897 42
6 The Hunt Ball, John Leech 48
7 St Paul's Church Deptford, used with permission of Lewisham Local History and Archives Centre 51
8 Charterhouse School 1805 53
9 Lady Wanton's Reputation in Danger, George Cruikshank 57
10 Feeding the Swans 64
11 Some Christmas Faces, Illustrated Times 69
12 Dinner Dress 1826, Ackermann's Repository of Arts 71
13 The Proposal, John Leech 75
14 Wedding Dress, Ackermann's Repository of Arts, January 1827 81
15 Mistley Church 83
16 The Quay at Dover, 1829 95
17 The French Fans, 1835, Courier des Salons 108
18 The Regatta, T. Alken 112
19 The Bath House on the Beach at Dawlish 115
20 A Fashionable Wedding, London Illustrated News 117
21 German Railway Station, 1841 119
22 Map of Konigswinter 121
23 The View from the Drachenfels 126
24 Coming Home, W. Morris 141
25 The Illustrated London News, July 23 1864 150
26 Mary Anointing the Feet of Jesus by Rubens 156
27 Very good; Very good indeed! 160
28 Christmas Time by Miss E. Osbourne, 1865 164
29 Exmouth from Louisa Terrace 170
30 Dressing for the Ball, The Graphic, 1870 172

Note that all illustrations are part of a private collection of antique prints except for those duly acknowledged.

Bibliography

Agassiz, Lewis, *A Journey to Switzerland, and Pedestrian Tours in that Country*, (London: Smith, Elder and Co, Cornhill, 1833)

Barker, John, *Lewis Agassiz of Stour Lodge*, (London: 2013)

Cassell, Peter and Galpin, *Cassell's Household Guide to Every Department of Practical Life: Being a Complete Encyclopædia of Domestic and Social Economy*, (London: 1869)

Cleveland, David, *Manningtree and Mistley: The People, Trades and Industries Past and Present*, (Essex: Cleveland, 2012)

Cobbett, William, *Advice to Young Men, and (incidentally) to Young Women in the Middle and Higher Ranks of Life*, (London: 1829)

Conway, Derwent, *Switzerland: the South of France and the Pyrenees in 1830*, Volume 1, (Edinburgh: Constable and Co., 1831)

Downing, Sarah Jane, *Fashion in the Time of Jane Austen*, (Oxford: Shire 2010)

Flanders, Judith, *The Victorian House*, (Harper Perennial: London, 2003)

Fryer and Horlock, Mike, Bob, *Revisiting the Past, Maps and Images of Mistley, Manningtree and Lawford*, (Essex: R.J. Horlock, 2013)

Garwood, Ivan, *Mistley in the days of the Rigby's*, (Norfolk: Lucas Books, 2003)

Goodman, Ruth, *How to be a Victorian*, (London: Penguin, 2013)

Goodfellow, Florence, *Memories of Pioneer Life in British Columbia*, (Published privately in Washington: 1945)

Inglis, Lucy, *Georgian London, Into the Streets*, (London: Penguin, 2013)

Kavanagh, Julie, *Women of Christianity. Exemplary for Acts of Piety and Charity*, (New York: D Appleton and Company; 1869)

Kloester, Jennifer, *Georgette Heyer's Regency World*, (London: Arrow Books, 2005)

Le Faye, Deidre, *Jane Austen, The World of her Novels*, (London: Frances Lincoln Limited, 2002)

Murray, John, *A Glance at some of the beauties and sublimities of Switzerland*, (London: Longman, 1829)

Phegley, Jennifer, *Courtship and Marriage in Victorian England*, (Oxford: Praeger, 2012)

Shelley, Mary Wollstonecraft, Percy Bysshe, *History of a Six Weeks' Tour through a Part of France, Switzerland, Germany and Holland*, (London: Hookham and Ollier, 1817)

Steinbach, Susie, *Women in England 1760 - 1914: A Social History*, (London: Phoenix, 2004)

Surtees, Virginia, Editor, *A Second Self: the Letters of Harriet Granville: 1810 - 1845*, (Salisbury: Michael Russell Publishing, 1990)

Vickery, Amanda, *The Gentleman's Daughter*, (London: Yale University Press, 1999)

Notes

Chapter 1

[1] In 1791, the disgraceful state of Upper Ground came to notice of parliament and a commissioner was appointed to oversee its improvement. Act 31 Geo Cap 61.
[2] Horwood's Map of London 1799 is accessible at www.motco.com. Nicholson's Yard is located at the bottom edge of sheet D2.
[3] John Barker, *Lewis Agassiz of Stour Lodge* (London: 2013).
[4] Julie Kavanagh, *Women of Christianity. Exemplary for Acts of Piety and Charity*, (New York: D Appleton and Company; 1869), p 10.
[5] Lewis Agassiz, *A Journey to Switzerland, and Pedestrian Tours in that Country*, (London: Smith, Elder and Co, Cornhill, 1833)
[1] Robert Nicholson's Will: National Archives Reference: PROB 11/1344/120. Proven 20 June 1800.
[2] A staunch Methodist and close friend of John Wesley's, Wolff was executor of Wesley's estate also.
[3] Frederick Nicholson was apprenticed to William Rolfe: London Metropolitan Archives; Reference Number: COL/CHD/FR/02/1315-1321.
[4] James Henry Nicholson was apprenticed to Richard Allen: National Archives: Apprenticeship Books: IR1: Piece 37. According to Holden's Triennial Directory 1805, Richard Allen was a Medical Doctor with premises at 60 High Street Southwark
[5] Robert Nicholson's first business premises was on the corner of King Street and Borough High Street, London Metropolitan Archives Reference: MPS 506130100
[6] Robert and Sarah Nicholson were married at St George's in the East, Shadwell, by license on 24 December 1774. Sarah was baptised in 1747 at St Olave's Church Hart St. She had an elder brother Thomas, the same age as Robert, who was also baptised there. Thomas Hawes, when he died in 1791, was buried in the new vault under the vestry at St Olave's Church. John Barnes, Robert's childhood friend, a baker in nearby Wapping, stood as a witness at their wedding.
[7] Robert and Sarah Nicholson's Children:
Robert was born 23 September 1775, baptised 4 October at St George the Martyr, buried 14 October 1775. Sarah Hawes was born 27 November, baptised 2 December 1776 at St George the Martyr. She was buried 29 March 1817 Plaistow, Kent. Ann was born about 1777. She was probably baptised at St Saviour's Denmark Place, Southwark. Unfortunately the baptism records for St Saviour's are difficult to read up until the year 1784. Robert was born in 1778. He was buried December 1799, aged 21 years at St Paul's Church, Deptford. Frederick was born in 1779 but not christened at St George's either. He died in 1820, Christchurch, Southwark. James Henry was born around 1780. He was buried St Paul's Deptford on 12 March 1802. George was baptised 16 April 1784 at St Saviour's Denmark Place, Southwark and was buried 21 December 1784 at St George the Martyr. Harriot was born around 1785, she died in 1867. Amelia was born 1786. She married Edward Creasy an auctioneer. William was baptised 5 September 1787 at St Saviour's and buried 27 March 1788 at St George the Martyr. Joseph was baptised 1788 at St Saviour's and buried 16 September 1789 at St George the Martyr. Louisa was baptised 28 December 1792 at St Saviour's. She married William Edmund Rolfe on 5 October in 1808. She died at the age of thirty in 1822 and was buried at St Paul's also. Edward was baptised 19 November 1794 and buried 14 November 1799 at St Paul's Deptford.

[8] Lewisham Archive Centre: A97/21/M58.
[9] Gibson had initially purchased six acres of farmland called Broom Close in 1766 in the Parish of Deptford, adding a further field to the holding before building on it in 1771.
[10] After Sarah's death, *The Morning Post*, 4 April 1821, advertised the property for sale: "A very desirable FREEHOLD ESTATE, pleasantly situated on that gentle acclivity, Loam Pitt [sic] Hill, Lewisham Road, consisting of a spacious stone-built Mansion, surrounded by about seven acres of Land, pleasingly diversified, and judiciously disposed in lawn, pleasure ground, full-grown plantations and productive -walled garden. The house is of respectable appearance, with portico to the principal front, is placed at an agreeable remove from the road and commands interesting and extensive prospects; it contains a large saloon, drawing, dining and breakfast rooms, library, seven bed chambers and very ample offices, coach house, stabling &c.; the whole conveniently arranged, and forming a very commodious and attractive residence, and also presenting an eligible opportunity for building upon, as the Estate possesses a frontage of 700 feet and contains good rich earth and chalk. See also *The Times*, July 22 1836 and 1 May 1824.
[11] Robert's funeral was held at St Paul's Deptford, on 5 June 1800.
[12] *The Times*, 4 December 1800.
[13] *Gentleman's Magazine and Historical Chronicles*, Volume 88, p 689 and also Volume 70, part 1 p 592, 1800.

Chapter 2
[1] Essex Records Office: Registry of Baptisms for Wix. He was born 17 December 1778 at Wix, baptised 20 December 1778.
[2] Golding Constable was a corn miller at East Bergholt. His business operated out of Mistley. His son John was three years older than Thomas Nunn (jun.). John Constable was expected to remain at home to work as a clerk in his father's office which he did until he persuaded his father to allow him to attend art school in 1799.
[3] The sons of several other bankers had set a precedent for this and been amply rewarded in their endeavours. Samson Hanbury from Coggeshall, Essex served on the Court of Assistants at the same time. Hanbury's father, a banker, had set his son up as a partner in Truman's Brewery in Spitalfields, ten years prior to Thomas Nunn arriving in the city. The Hanbury's, living near Colchester, were also involved in hunts with the Nunn family.
[4] The 'dealership in porter and bottled ales' with George Whitehead of nearby Round Street ended in 1804: *London Gazette,* March 25 1804, p 1258.
[5] Guildhall Library CLC/L/BF/B/001/MS05445/032, p492: The Minute Books of the Worshipful Company of Brewers.
[6] He was admitted a Freeman by Redemption on 8 October 1802. He paid seven pounds for the privilege.
[7] 15 April 1803. Information supplied by the archivist at the Brewers Hall, London. Confirmed by the minute books of the Brewers Company, MS05445/033, p 5.
[8] Jennifer Kloester, *Georgette Heyer's Regency World*, (London: Arrow Books, 2005), p106.
[9] Amanda Vickery, *The Gentleman's Daughter*, (London: Yale University Press, 1999), p 86.
[10] George Wolff was a signatory to the marriage settlement between George and Mary Bridges. The Bridges lived in Lawford Place, next door to Lawford House.
[11] Jane Austen, *Pride and Prejudice,* first published 1813. Chapter 1.
[12] Jane Austen, *Pride and Prejudice,* Chapter 13.
[13] Essex Records Office: D/DQ 37/50 3 February 1803. Sarah Nicholson, Thomas Nunn Senior and Carrington Nunn were signatories to a marriage settlement of £5000 upon the couple, as had been determined by Ann's father in his will.
[14] Ann Nicholson and Thomas Nunn were married on 3 February 1803.
[15] At Number 46 Red Cross Street, Thomas and Ann Nunn's home was just opposite the home of Thomas Nunn's Essex acquaintance, William Tomlins. Essex Records Office: D/DHwT122. Tomlins was a baker of Red Cross Street, London who leased mills in Lawford.
[16] Dr William's Library was next door to the Nunn residence. It was a nonconformist theological library which held a valuable collection of manuscripts including a copy of Shakespeare's first folio.

[17] The Peacock Brewery was the most productive one in the country forty years before. By Thomas's time it had larger competitors. Thomas owned a joint partnership in this brewery with the Calvert family. The Peacock Brewery was wound up in 1810. Thomas Nunn moved house at the same time. Thomas did not appear at the Company of Brewer's meetings after the end of that year. Within two years the plant was sold and the brewery's buildings had been demolished and rebuilt as a debtor's prison. The Calvert family continued their enterprise elsewhere.

[18] Virginia Surtees Editor, *A Second Self: the Letters of Harriet Granville: 1810 – 1845*, (Michael Russell Publishing: Salisbury, 1990), p 84.

[19] Sarah Eliza was born in Streatham according to the 1871 census. Perhaps she was born at Balham House, the country home of George Wolff. It is more likely though that Ann was in Lewisham for her confinement. Particularly since that is where she was buried, just four months after Sarah Eliza's birth.

[20] Deptford Records Centre burial records: Ann Nunn was buried on 10 June 1806 at St Paul's Deptford.

[21] Essex Records Office: The Manorial Records of Lawford Hall. 4 October 1808: Admission of Thomas Nunn Junior for the sum of £1825 to the farm of Wisdoms, Millers and Whiting's. It was just to the west of his father's Lawford House Farm. He purchased a further forty acres in 1811 on the Mistley side of Lawford.

Chapter 3

[1] John Constable: 'The Bridges Family, 1804'.

[2] John Constable had spent a while moving around the neighbourhood painting portraits of local farmer's families, only charging a few guineas for each.
http://www.tate.org.uk/art/artworks/constable-the-bridges-family-n06130/text-catalogue-entry

[3] Thomas Nunn (sen.) referred to the portraits of his family as belonging in the dining room of Lawford House in his will of 1834.

[4] George Bridges was Nunn's closest neighbour, living across the road from him at Lawford Place. Bridges had purchased part of the Dales Hall property in 1796. George Bridges with his father and uncle were Mistley-based merchants trading in coal, corn, timber and iron. Their ships plied the route between London and Mistley. With John Marratt, George Bridges had founded the Manningtree and Mistley Bank in 1790, then Hadleigh Bank in 1799. The Harwich branch was added in 1812. John Bridges, George's father lived in the large mansion next to the Mistley Thorn Inn for many years. He, along with Thomas Nunn (sen.) was a Justice of the Peace and a magistrate for Mistley.

[5] George Bridges and his partner had undertaken a twenty-one year lease of the port of Mistley in 1811 but they suffered in the slump that followed the war with France. He pulled out of his bank in 1815 and sold his home at Lawford Place the following year in 1816. He removed his family to Knightsbridge in London. At the same time, his eldest son and heir eloped with his bride to Gretna Green. When the couple returned home to London they were remarried at St George's, Hanover Square, the most fashionable wedding venue in London. Then the couple settled in Jamaica.

[6] Samuel Taylor Coleridge described his son Hartley's breeching ceremony in 1801 in a letter to his friend Robert Southey:
He ran to and fro in a sort of dance to the Jingle of the Load of Money that had been put in his breeches pockets; but he did [not] roll and tumble over in his old joyous way – No! It was an eager and solemn gladness as if he felt it to be an awful era in his life. O bless him! Bless him! Bless him! Robert Southey's son was later to become young Thomas's brother-in-law when his half-sister Henrietta Nunn married Rev Charles Cuthbert Southey in 1853.

[7] Carrington Nunn, Thomas's brother was born at Wix on 28 October 1780. He was buried 25 December 1863 aged 83. He ran the Essex Union Pack and became master of the Suffolk and Essex Hounds. Carrington kept the pack of hounds for the hunt for fifty years. According to *Baileys Magazine of Sports and Pastimes*: Volume 26 1875, p 375, he was "a capital sportsman."

[8] Carrington Nunn's hounds were taken over by his nephew Thomas in 1849 according to the *Chelmsford Chronicle* of 11 May 1849.

[9] London Metropolitan Archives CLC/B/192/F/001/MS11936/430/752752

Chapter 4
[1] Pigot's Trade Directory for Essex 1832-1833. Wheat was then known as corn.
[2] In the Rigby family's survey of Mistley 1778 Thomas Nunn (sen.) held Bradfield Lodge and Wix Lodge. Will of Joseph Nunn D/ABW 108/1/35. Joseph Nunn was buried 12 April 1782 at Mistley after his death.
[3] CLC/B/192/F/001/MS11936/391/605705 Royal and Sun Alliance Insurance records at London Metropolitan Archives show an estate valued at £2750.
[4] Essex Record Office: D/DFI T23 William purchased Nether Hall and Dickley Hall. Robert purchased parts of Dale Hall Farm.
[5] John Hanson was of a London mercantile family. He moved back to London with his family in 1808 saying in his notes that the society was not what he wished his children to associate with as they grew older.
[6] Essex Records Office: T/B442 In John Hanson's biographical work he writes that he purchased Great Bromley Hall in 1792, "little anticipating that it was soon to become the centre post of a large Garrison and indeed the headquarters of a Great Army to defend Essex against the threatened invasion of a ferocious enemy."
[7] Hanson wrote the song for the presentation of colours ceremony in 1798. Essex Records Office Reference: D/DHa 01/20.
[8] Essex Records Office: L/O 3/2 13.
[9] Ownership of land in the appropriate county, worth at least £200 per year, was the requirement to qualify for the appointment. *A Compendious Abstract of the Public General Acts of the United Kingdom of Great Britain and Ireland*, J.W. Paget. Volumes 5-9, (Google eBook) Great Britain. Carrington was still fulfilling his role as a Deputy Lieutenant in 1852. *Essex Standard* 17 September 1852, p2.
[10] Essex Records Office: D/DaF5/1
[11] Bailey's Magazine of Sports and Pastimes, Volume 26 1875, page 375. 'Then Mr Carrington Nunn and his brother Tom, better known as Hat Nunn were masters...'

Chapter 5
[1] Harriot married James Dowley in 1805 and Amelia married a land agent, Edward Hill Creasy in 1807.
[2] *A Second Self*, p 42.
[3] Essex Record Office: L/O 3/2 13
[4] In 1814, the partnership was reformed when Thomas Nunn (jun.) replaced Grace Marratt and the Mills family
[5] Guildhall Library CLC/L/BF/B/001/MS05445/033, p388: The Minute Books of the Worshipful Company of Brewers. Thomas Nunn was surprised when he received notification from the Court of Assistants that he was to be appointed Renter Warden for the year. In response he refused to attend the court since he lived so far away and he also declined to pay the obligatory fine that would fall to him if he declined the office. He felt it would make too large a dent in his purse!

Chapter 6
[1] John Constable's mother wrote to her son of the 'Grand dance at Mr Bridges, Lawford' on 18 January 1811. Accessed online at http://www.tate.org.uk/art/artworks/constable-the-bridges-family-n06130/text-catalogue-entry. Peter Godfrey was the Lord of the Manor at Old Hall.
[2] John Hannavy, *Encyclopedia of Nineteenth-century Photography*, Volume 1, (London: Taylor and Francis, 2008), p211.
[3] Lawford Place was purchased by Richard Cox, Thomas Nunn's banking partner.
[4] National Archives: ADM 101/112/1/7 John Moor of Mistley served as a corporal in the Royal Marines at the same time as Lewis Agassiz.
[5] Elizabeth was married to Isaac Phillebrown, a merchant of Mistley, for seventeen years before he died in 1816.
[6] Marianne Mount was baptised on 5 June, 1785, at Wapping. She married John Sacket Ayles in 1803. He died in 1813. Her parents were Elizabeth and Richard Mount and her brothers were Richard and William. She was one of eight daughters. Marianne and Thomas married

on 7 February 1820 when Sarah Eliza was fourteen. Their marriage settlement had been drawn up six months prior to this and was dated 23 September 1819.
[7] 11 December 1821 was Mary Nunn's date of burial at Mistley Church.
[8] Sarah Nicholson was buried 4 December 1820 at St Paul's Deptford. Her will was brief, dated 18 Nov 1820. She referred to three daughters, Harriot, Amelia, Louisa, and Frederick's wife now a widow, but made no mention of Thomas Nunn or his children.
[9] Matilda Nunn, daughter of Thomas and Mary Ann was baptised at Leyton on 25 August 1822. She was born at Mistley on 8 June that year. Henrietta Elizabeth was baptised February 18 1824, at Mistley.
[10] Essex Record Office: T/B442, the autobiographical notes of John Hanson.
[11] Carrington Nunn aged four months died as an infant and was buried at Mistley on 2 April 1825.
[12] Essex Record Office: Registers for St John the Baptist Church, Loughton. Lewis Robert Agassiz was baptised 28 March 1818. St Mary's, Mistley Burial Registers: 18 July 1818.
[13] Mary Ann married John Ayles 4 September 1824, aged 21, at St Mary's, Mistley.
[14] Essex Record Office: Elizabeth Agassiz died on 28 December 1825. She was buried at the Church of St Mary the Virgin, Mistley on 4 January 1826 according to the burial registers.

Chapter 7
[1] Meteorology@West Moors,
accessed online at http://booty.org.uk/booty.weather/climate/1800_1849.htm
[2] *The Times,* Wednesday 16 June, 1828. This article about a robbery provides evidence that Thomas Nunn lived in Mistley. Also there are various pieces of correspondence that list him as Thomas Nunn of Mistley.
[3] The Ayles resided at New Hall, Beaumont. *Morning Chronicle,* 18 February 1828, p4.
[4] The first English translation of *Grimm's Fairy Tales* was published in 1823, the same year that *The Night before Christmas* was penned.
[5] Robert Ackermann, *The Repository of Arts, Literature, Fashions &C.* Third Series, Volume 9, Number XLIV, January 1827
[6] Jennifer Phegley, *Courtship and Marriage in Victorian England,* (Oxford: Praeger, 2012), p 27.
[7] Essex Records Office: D/ACL 1827 Thomas Nunn settled £4000 on his daughter in 3% consols. This would have provided Sarah Eliza with an independent income of £120 per annum.
[8] Essex Records Office: D/ACL 1827 Marriage Licence applied for 14 Feb 1827.

Chapter 8
[1] Eliza enjoyed only two days of legal independence between attaining twenty-one and becoming married. Upon marriage, a woman came under the legal title of 'femmes covert'; she was completely represented by her husband under law until the 1870s. She could not sign a contract or make a will without her husband's verification and she held no legal standing in court. Jennifer Phegley, *Courtship and Marriage in Victorian England,* p 17.
[2] William Cobbett, *Advice to Young Men, and (incidentally) to Young Women in the Middle and Higher Ranks of Life,* (London: 1829), p 97.
[3] Harriot Dowley was the only one of Ann's siblings still alive. She remained in Southwark. Sarah Hawes Dowley died in 1817; Frederick was no longer alive by the time of his mother's death in 1820 according to Sarah Nicholson's will. Louisa Rolfe died in 1822 at Lewisham. Amelia Creasy died in Brighton in 1824.

Chapter 9
[1] 'Pale-maille is a game wherein a round box ball is struck with a mallet through a high arch of iron, which he that can do at the fewest blows, or at the number agreed upon, wins.' Joseph Strutt *The Sports and Pastimes of the People of England,* (London: Methven and Company 1801), p 98.
[2] *Essex Standard* 18 May 1833 p 1. In the Auction of Household Goods, the yellow moreen curtains were described as 'new'.

[3] In the same article, The Auction of Household Goods, *Essex Standard* 18 May 1833 p 1.
[4] 'No food is so congenial to the child as the milk of its own mother; its quality is made by nature to suit the age of the child; it comes with the child and is calculated precisely for its stomach.' William Cobbett, *Advice to Young Men.* p 101.
[5] Amanda Vickery, *The Gentleman's Daughter: Women's Lives in Georgian England*, (London: Yale University Press, 1998), p 98.
[6] *The Gentleman's Daughter,* p 96.
[7] Peter Cassell, *Cassell's Household Guide to Every Department of Practical Life: Being a Complete Encyclopædia of Domestic and Social Economy*, (London: 1869).
[8] Robert was buried on 13 June 1828 at St Mary's Mistley.
[9] Arthur was born on 24 December 1828.
[10] Of nursery assistants: William Cobbett (*Advice to Young Men,* p 271) informed young parents: "Let them be *assistants* in the most strict sense of the word... let children never be *left to them alone.*"

Chapter 10

[1] Lewis Agassiz, *A Journey to Switzerland, and Pedestrian Tours in that Country*, (London: Smith, Elder and Co, Cornhill, 1833), p 22. Cousin Arthur lived with his wife and children at Chateau de Bossey near Nyon. Lewis Agassiz, *A Journey to Switzerland, and Pedestrian Tours in that Country,* (London: Smith, Elder and Co, Cornhill, 1833), p 22.
[2] Mary Wollstonecraft Shelley, Percy Bysshe Shelley, *History of a Six Weeks' Tour through a Part of France, Switzerland, Germany and Holland*, (London: Hookham and Ollier, 1817).
[3] David Lewis Agassiz was baptised on 12 July 1737, the son of Jean Pierre Moise Agassiz of Bavois, Switzerland.
[4] Derwent Conway, *Switzerland: the South of France and the Pyrenees in 1830, Volume 1,* (Edinburgh: Constable and Co., 1831), p 268.
[5] He mentioned Bruges as a destination when he applied for leave from the marines. The National Archives: ADM 6/141.
[6] Lewis and Eliza may have visited Deptford because Lewis mentions it, if rather disparagingly in his book, p233.
[7] *A Journey to Switzerland,* p 2.
[8] Ibid. p 5.
[9] Ibid. p 36.
[10] Ibid. p 12.
[11] Ibid. p 47.
[12] Ibid. p 119.
[13] John Murray, *A Glance at some of the beauties and sublimities of Switzerland,* (London: Longman, 1829), p 52.
[14] *A Journey to Switzerland,* p 116.
[15] *A Journey to Switzerland,* p 268.
[16] Eliza Louisa Susanna Vaudine was born on 16 August 1830.
[17] They departed on 15 October 1830.
[18] *A Journey to Switzerland,* p 266.

Chapter 11

[1] Mary Anne Ayles was born early February 1828, and baptised on 9 April 1828 at Beaumont Cum Mose. John Mount Ayles was born 14 October 1829, baptised at Beaumont on January 26 1830. The birth of Louisa Sophie followed in 1831. She was baptised at Beaumont Cum Mose on 28 June 1831.
[2] The Agassiz's third son, Rodolph, was born on 16 January 1832 in Bradfield 17 months after Vaudine was born in Switzerland.
[3] *Essex Standard,* Saturday 21 January 1832, p 3.
[4] Susie Steinbach, *Women in England 1760 - 1914, A Social History,* (London: Phoenix, 2004), p 44.
[5] *Essex Standard,* Saturday 18 August 1832, p 3.
[6] *Essex Standard,* Saturday 15 September 1832, p 1.

[7] Colonel Cook, *Observations on Fox-hunting and the Management of Hounds in the Kennel and the Field,* (London: William Nichol, 1826) Along with Thomas Nunn, Carrington Nunn and John Ayles, Lewis subscribed to this book.
[8] John Ayles of Beaumont also auctioned his possessions at this time. The Ayles family moved into Mistley, to the house next to the Mistley Thorn.
[9] Mary Ann Agassiz was born in Mannheim on 28 February 1834.
[10] National Archives Reference: Will of Thomas Nunn (sen.) PROB 11/2259/44
[11] The records at the Stadtarchive Mannheim note that Lewis had left Mannheim by 22 December 1834.
[12] In December 1837, the *Essex Standard* was still running an invitation from Lewis's solicitor for any creditors to come forward to make their claim on the estate of Robert Nunn.
[13] Thomas Griesdale Agassiz was born on 18 January 1836. Lewis registered his new son's birth in the company of Thomas Nunn's friend of his youth, George Way and a young army captain, Frederic Brandreth who was on his Grand Tour.
[14] Susie Steinbach, *Women in England 1760 - 1914, A Social History,* (London: Phoenix, 2004), p 44.
[15] *Exeter and Plymouth Gazette* 3 January 1835, p 2. Mr Agassiz was steward at the Annual Christmas and Juvenile Ball at Dawlish, *Western Times* 21 January 1837 p3. *Western Times,* 29 July 1837, Lewis Agassiz was a steward at the Dawlish Regatta.
[16] Thomas Griesdale Agassiz died on 21 January 1840.
[17] *Exeter Western Times,* 18 September 1840, p 2.
[18] Essex Records Office: Mistley Baptism Register: October 17, 1840.
[19] *Exeter and Plymouth Gazette,* 19 December 1840, p3.

Chapter 12
[1] *The Morning Post,* 1 March 1841, p1 and 16 October 1843, p1.
[2] The connection had been in operation since 1837.
[3] Roland, Eliza's ninth child, was born on 21 April 1841 in Cologne. *A Short History of the English Branch,* p.32. He was privately baptised in 1842. Essex Records Centre, Bradfield Register. He was admitted to the Bradfield congregation in 1847 when Eleanor and Edward were baptised.
[4] The rail connection further on to Bonn was not completed until 1844.
[5] The Shelley's *History of a Six Weeks Tour,* p 69.
[6] William Shakespeare's *King Lear,* Act 3, scene 4.
[7] Eleanor Eliza Agassiz was born 30 December, 1842 according to *A Short History of the English Branch* but the birth was registered at Konigswinter in December 1841 according to John Barker, *Lewis Agassiz of Stour Lodge.*
[8] John Ayles occupation changed from being that of a gentleman to being a wine merchant in the baptismal records of his children that were born between 1840 and 1850. Thomas Nunn (jun.) loaned him the finance to set up the dealership.
[9] John Murray, *A Glance at Some of the Beauties and Sublimities of Switzerland,* (London: Longman, 1829), p43.
[10] Internet Reference: *www.anatpro.com/index_files/William_Harper_Brandreth.htm*
[11] Her second child, Frederic Lewis was born on 23 October 1843 in Winchester where her husband had been posted with his company. She died on 6 November. *The Hampshire Chronicle* 13 November 1843.
[12] Birth registration: Standesampt Königswinter. James Albert was born on 3 July 1844. Arthur Rodolph Nunn Agassiz, *A Short History of the English Branch of the Agassiz Family.*
[13] Florence Goodfellow mentions their friendship in her autobiographical essay *Memories of Pioneer Life in British Columbia,* (Washington: 1945) p 5.
[14] The villa took the name of its new owner, Hubert Schauffhausen. A picture of Villa Schauffhausen may be viewed online at http://de.wikipedia.org/wiki/Villa_Schaaffhausen
[15] In 1847 he called a national assembly to begin the process of unification. The Prussian War began in earnest in 1848 but Eliza, Lewis and their family had long departed and were settled in peaceful Essex by that time.
[16] *Essex Standard,* Friday 7 August 1846, p 3.

[17] *The Hampshire Chronicle*, 24 August 1844. *The Morning Post*, 17 April 1847 records his later promotion to First Lieutenant. Young Lewis Nunn had set his heart on a military career by the time he turned sixteen. The King of Prussia offered him a commission in the Prussian forces but the family declined.
[18] *Chelmsford Chronicle*, 18 September 1846.
[19] *Chelmsford Chronicle*, 4 June 1847.
[20] Edward Albert Agassiz was born at Bradfield on 24 November, 1846.
[21] *Ipswich Journal*, 14 April 1849, p8.
[22] *Ipswich Journal*, 29 June 1849, p8.

Chapter 13
[1] *Barclay's Complete and Universal English Dictionary*, 1842, quoted at www.genuki.org.uk
[2] The homes of Colleton Crescent were built in 1802.
[3] Numerous newspaper advertisements that advertised the property mention the outstanding views. For example, *The Exeter and Plymouth Gazette*, Sunday 5 November 1848, p 8.
[4] Elizabeth Ann Agassiz was born on 21 March 1850.
[5] They resided at 7 St James Place which has now been renamed Old Tiverton Road.
[6] James David and Louisa Agassiz still lived in Dawlish at 16 Queen Street according to the 1851 census.
[7] They were married 9 October 1828 in Frome, Somerset.
[8] Devon Records Office: 48/28/33/1-10. Jane's will reveals hints of her sharp tongue and a tendency to criticism.
[9] 1851 Census, Exeter Holy Trinity District 5B: Frederic Carrington 13, Alfred, 11, Roland 10, were all scholars. Eleanor, Fredreich Wilhelm and Albert Edward were scholars at home.
[10] The local grammar school was situated less than half a mile away in High Street.
[11] Mrs. Beeton's recipe calls for 2 tbsp Curry Powder, 6 onions, 1 clove garlic, 1 oz ground almonds, 1 fowl or rabbit, 4 slices of lean bacon, and 2 quarts stock.
[12] Richard Cannon, *Historical Record of the Twenty-third Regiment or the Royal Welsh Fusiliers,* printed by authority: London, 1850, pages 158 -163. The battalion was in Trinidad before they arrived in Halifax, Nova Scotia in 1847. Then they were stationed at Winchester from September 1848 until April 1850 when they proceeded to Plymouth before embarking for Canada later in the year.
[13] National Archives: ADM 36/17135. James David joined his father and brother on *HMS Rattler* in 1807 aged six.
[14] Archery was a sport that was considered acceptable for women to participate in. James David and Louisa were keen on the hobby. *Exeter Flying Post,* 4 September 1856; *Western Times* Saturday 12 September, 1857. Eliza later sold her bow in a sale of household effects. *Essex Standard,* Friday 8 March 1870.
[15] James John Charles only had two surviving sons, James David and Lewis, half-brothers, each the progeny of the wives who preceded Jane.
[16] *Prince Edward Island Royal Gazette*, 21 May 1850, p 3.
[17] Florence Goodfellow, daughter of Lewis Nunn Agassiz wrote *Memories of Pioneer Life in British Columbia*. (Published privately in Washington: 1945), p 6.
[18] Devon Record Office: Dawlish Burial Register. The Death Certificate provides the information that an inflammation of the chest was the cause of death on 9 September 1850.
[19] *Prince Edward Island Examiner*, 12 May 1851. p 35.
[20] *Western Times* 29 May 1853, p 6.
[21] John Mount Ayles was a Captain for Green's Company.
[22] In 1853 Fred was a midshipman aboard *HM Merchant Ship Anglesey*. National Archives Record: Seaman's Ticket 565,366.
[23] Florence Goodfellow, *Memories of Pioneer Life in British Columbia*. p 6.
[24] Ibid. 24 March 1852
[25] Ibid. Arthur Agassiz was born 14 February 1853. p 7.
[26] *Exeter and Plymouth Gazette*, Saturday 23 November 1850.
[27] Edward John Tilt, *The Change of Life, in Health and Disease,* (Philadelphia: Blakiston, 1871), p 44.
[28] *Exeter and Plymouth Gazette,* dated 12 April 1856.

Chapter 14

[1] Thomas Nunn's Death Certificate records that he died of an erysipelas infection combined with old age on 7 March 1857.
[2] Thomas Nunn's Will: National Archives: Prerogative Court of Canterbury Will Registers: PROB 11/2259.
[3] Thomas Nunn's Will: PROB 11/2259.
[4] James John Charles Agassiz died on 16 December 1857 of old age.
[5] Devon Record Office: The will of James John Charles Agassiz.
[6] *Essex Standard*, Friday 9 July 1858.
[7] National Archives Service Record ADM/196/60
[8] America was in the midst of gold rush fever. Pike's Peak in Colorado was discovered in 1858. There was also gold-mining in New Mexico.
[9] US Federal Census 1860: San Miguel Division: M653-713, p123. His enlistment papers show that he arrived in New Mexico via Memphis.
[10] *London Daily News,* Thursday 22 January, 1863, p 5.
[11] On the night of the 1861 census only Vaudine, aged 30, and Friedrich Wilhelm, aged 17, were home. Mary Ann and Eleanor were visiting their aunt in Dedham.
[12] *Essex Standard*, 30 May 1866, p 4.
[13] *Essex Standard*, 30 August 1861, p 3. They were married 28 August 1861 by Rev. W. Frost assisted by the Rev. Dr. Hayne, the parish vicar.
[14] *Essex Standard*, Friday 15 July 1864, p 3. "Reports have been very currently circulated as to the "rotten" [sic] condition of the sleepers, but this is a great exaggeration."
[15] Margaret Hayle was the wife of the Rev. Dr. Hayle, Rector of Bradfield and Mistley from 1860 to 1871. She was a similar age to Eliza. She died in 1874 in Devon. *Chelmsford Chronicle* 20 March 1874 p 8.
[16] *Essex Standard*, Friday 15 July 1864, p 3. "Help soon arrived from the village, the Rector, Rev. Dr. Hayne being among the earliest and he at once conducted the passengers to the Rectory where they received the kindest attention."

Chapter 15

[1] Lewis Agassiz died 23 April 1866.
[2] U.S Army, Register of Enlistments, accessed at www.ancestry.com. By coincidence Frederic Carrington resigned (deserted) on 17 January 1866. (This may have been in response to his mother informing him of his Father's ill health).
[3] Essex Records Office: D/DBm T54 Contains Lewis Agassiz's will and also some letters between the solicitor's office and Eliza regarding the valuation of Stour Lodge and the fees incurred.
[4] *Essex Standard*, 19 September 1866.
[5] *Ipswich Journal*, 1 December 1866; *Essex Standard*, 30 May 1866.

Chapter 16

[1] Frederic Brandreth married Jane Gandy in 1846 after his first wife Elizabeth Mary Ann died. When she came into her inheritance he took the name of Gandy by Royal License in 1852.
[2] *Essex Standard*, Wednesday 12 December 1866.
[3] Jeanette Amy Vaudine Ayles was baptised on August 18 1862 at Bradfield. John James Lewis was baptised there on June 18, 1864 as was Frederick Norman on February 18 1866. Fanny Eleanor Vandira was also baptised at Bradfield on February 16, 1867, though her father was resident in Kent.
[4] John Mount Ayles married Elizabeth Julia Thorne on 15 February 1868, in the parish of Hackney, St John.
[5] Ferney Coombe became the Canadian community that bears the family name of Agassiz.
[6] Florence Goodfellow, p 19.
[7] Florence Goodfellow, p 21.
[8] Florence Goodfellow, p 22.
[9] He married Mary Louisa Davis, in Plymouth. She was the granddaughter of Lieutenant Colonel George Lennox Davis. *Cork Examiner,* 19 April 1852, reports his death in Ireland.

[10] *Essex Standard,* Friday 26 June 1863.
[11] *Ipswich Journal,* 16 November 1867.
[12] *Essex Standard,* 12 February 1869.
[13] *Essex Standard,* 29 April 1870, p2.
[14] *Worcestershire Chronicle,* 27 July 1870, p 4.
[15] Those photos remain in the possession of family members to this day. Some were published in John Barker's, *Lewis Agassiz of Stour Lodge.*
[16] *Essex Standard,* Friday 5 March 1869. Stour Lodge was said to be 3 minute walk from the station and a quarter mile from the Bradfield Church. The advertisement also claimed that the house had seven lofty bedrooms. This suggests that Lewis must have expanded it over the years from the initial four bedrooms.
[17] *Essex Standard,* 12 November 1870. In November 1870 the house was undergoing major renovations under the hands of its new owner.

Chapter 17
[1] *Essex Standard,* 14 June 1872. The household goods went into storage for a time. Eighteen months later an auction of the contents of the family house was held. The auction included archery targets and bows as well as croquet balls and mallets.
[2] Devon Record Office: St Thomas, Devonshire Folio 5b/p 25. Louisa Wentworth Stackpoole Agassiz died in December, 1861 leaving her husband the £14,000 she had inherited from her family estate.
[3] Death Certificate: St Thomas, Exmouth, Devon. James David Agassiz was aged 70 years. He suffered from hypertrophy of the heart, hemiplegia and gout as well as a chronic enlargement of the prostate gland.
[4] Devon Record Office: St Thomas, Devonshire Folio 5b/p 39.
[5] Devon Record Office: Will of James David Agassiz.
[6] Jane Agassiz died on 4 December 1871 according to the National Probate Calendar.
[7] Devon Record Office: 3 48/28/33/1-10 Jane altered her will to leave Eliza £200.
[8] *Exeter and Plymouth Gazette,* 22 September 1871.
[9] Mrs Waters and Mrs Abbot were also widows who lived in Louisa Terrace. 1871 Census for Littleham, Exmouth, District 3, p 11.
[10] *Essex Standard,* 5 April 1872.
[11] Henrietta Nunn Southey died on 8 December 1869. The Rev Southey had remarried by the time of Eleanor's wedding. His attendance indicates a continued close connection with his erstwhile sister-in-law, Eliza. At the time one of his daughter's appears to have been living next door to Eliza – see 1871 census.
[12] *Exeter and Plymouth Gazette,* 15 August 1873. The couple were married on August 12.
[13] *Pall Mall Gazette* 3 June 1874, p 3. Vaudine Jessie was born on May 13 1874.
[14] Friedrich resigned from the parish of Seaforth in Nova Scotia and returned to England in 1880. His family, which continued to grow, took up residence in Dover when he became a chaplain for the armed forces. Friedrich received recognition for serving under heavy fire in Egypt. *Chelmsford Chronicle,* 11 November 1882.
[15] This is family lore, a tale told by the great granddaughters of Fred that their grandmother had corresponded with a half-brother and half-sister who lived in the United States. There is no evidence of Fred's previous marriage in the United States except for the certificate of his marriage to Harriet in which he is identified as a widower. However there is a census record from Pettis Missouri 1870 of an Edmund Agassiz and wife Ellen with two children aged 4 and 2 which might be applicable to Fred, especially if he had indeed 'deserted' from his regiment. Additionally there is a Wisconsin State Census record of a Sister Goda Agassiz in 1905, who was born in 1870, Illinois, of English parents. This would tie in with the story that Fred's son and daughter became a nun and a priest in the Catholic Church.
[16] US Register of Enlistments 1798 – 1914: accessed at www.ancestry.com
[17] Florence Goodfellow, p 36. 'My English grandmother began to be very anxious to see my father, who was her eldest son,' Florence wrote in her memoirs.
[18] *Christchurch Press,* 19 November 1874, p 2.
[19] Frederick Carrington Agassiz married Harriet Elizabeth Hamilton on 24 November 1875. They had ten children.

[20] Harriet Agassiz was later to follow her mother-in-law's example and prepared delicately worked handkerchiefs for the wife of her grandson James Carrington Barnes on the occasion of their marriage.
[21] *Exeter and Plymouth Gazette* 25 August 1874.
[22] *Morning Post* 24 April 1875, p 5. *London Standard, 15 December 1881, p2*. Roland was promoted to Major.
[23] *Bury and Norwich Post*, Tuesday 17 August 1875, p3. Mary Ann Ayles died on 10 August 1875.
[24] *Bury and Norwich Post*, 1 August 1876, p 6. They married on 18 July 1876.
[25] *Western Gazette*, 20 December 1878. With Mrs Southey, at the piano, Edward and Maria entertained the audience at the Kingsbury Episcopalian Concert.
[26] *Western Times*, 20 February 1877, p 7.
[27] *Chelmsford Chronicle*, 27 August 1880 p 4.
[28] Eleanor died 25 March 1881 at 5 Waterfield Terrace, Blackheath. Death Certificate: Greenwich, Vol 1d, page 644.
[29] Kelly's Directory 1882. Mrs S.E. Agassiz lived at Whalley Villa, Shooter's Hill.
[30] *Exeter and Plymouth Gazette*, 20 May 1881.
[31] Including some by Luny and other masters.
[32] *The Hampshire Telegraph*, 24 June 1882, p 3. Mrs and Miss Agassiz from Blackheath were staying at 2 Southsea Terrace according to the Southsea Visitors List.
[33] National Archives: Service Record of Roland Lewis Agassiz
[34] *Essex Standard*, 12 April 1884.
[35] Essex Record Office D/P173/1/8.

Chapter 18

[1] She had forty-seven grandchildren at the time of her death. However, Eliza had enjoyed a close relationship with only a small portion. There were ten grandchildren living in British Columbia. They never met Eliza but they knew of her. Florence, Lewis Nunn's eldest daughter wrote of her English grandmother's parcels and letters in her memoirs, years later.
Rodolph and Mary had a family of eight. They were living in Camberwell, London at the time of Eliza's death. Their children enjoyed a close and enduring relationship with Eliza. The youngest, Lucien was ten at her passing.
Mary Ann, Eliza's remaining daughter had just celebrated her fiftieth birthday a few weeks before her mother's death. It is difficult to imagine how she might have felt at the time of her mother's passing. Mary Ann's youth had vanished caring for her family. She still felt a great bond with the east country and consequently she moved back to Essex. Mary Ann bought a property in Dedham where she could enjoy the company of her cousins, the Ayles spinsters. She continued to care for her nieces and nephew. Many of the family possessions were passed from Mary Ann to Eleanor's children. Some treasures remain in the possession of Eleanor's descendants to this day.
Frederic Carrington made a new life for himself in New Zealand. He and Harriet had a family of ten. Whether Fred ever spoke of his mother is unknown. There were only stories of his father's exploits handed down through the subsequent generations. Alfred, who had also settled in New Zealand, moved to Australia with a new wife, leaving his children with their relatives in New Zealand. Those children knew even less than Fred's of their English grandparents.
Roland continued to pursue his career in the marines, eventually achieving promotion to Lieutenant Colonel in 1887. When Roland retired he too lived in Dedham, near his sister. His own son, Thomas, was fourteen at the time of Eliza's death.
Friedrich Wilhelm and his wife Jessie had six children by the time Eliza died, three of them were born in Nova Scotia, the others in Dover. The family resided close enough to visit their grandmother in Greenwich in her later years. Two more children were born to the couple, before their marriage came to an end.
The youngest of Eliza's sons, Edward Albert, died the year after his mother's demise, leaving just one young son. Roland took care of him after his mother's death.
[2] Susan Steinbach, *Women in England 1760 - 1914: A Social History*, (Phoenix: London 2004), p 2.

Made in the USA
Lexington, KY
24 October 2014